Political Economy of Policy Reform in Developing Countries

The Ohlin Lectures

1. Jagdish Bhagwati, *Protectionism* (1988)

2. Richard N. Cooper, *Economic Stabilization and Debt in Developing Countries* (1992)

3. Assar Lindbeck, *Unemployment and Macroeconomics* (1993)

4. Anne O. Krueger, *Political Economy of Policy Reform in Developing Countries* (1993)

Political Economy of
Policy Reform in
Developing Countries

Anne O. Krueger

The MIT Press
Cambridge, Massachusetts
London, England

Third printing, 1995

© 1993 Massachusetts Institute of Technology

This book was set in Palatino by Maple-Vail Composition Services and was printed and bound in the United States of America.

Library of Congress Cataloging-in-Publication Data

Krueger, Anne O.
  Political economy of policy reform in developing countries / Anne O. Krueger.
  p. cm.—(The Ohlin lectures ; 4)
  Includes bibliographical references and index.
  ISBN 0-262-11178-0
  1. Developing countries—Economic policy. 2. Developing countries—Politics and government. 3. Developing countries—Commerce. I. Title. II. Series.
HC59.7.K753   1993   92-41790
338.9′009172′4—dc20   CIP

Contents

Preface   ix

1 Introduction   1

2 Economic Policies in Developing Countries   11
Across-the-board Economic Policy
Difficulties   13
Contrasting Economic Policies of the High
Flyers   29

3 Origins of Economic Policies   37
Initial Conditions under Which Economic Policy
Was Formulated   39
Ideas Underlying Industrialization in Developing
Countries   43
Role of Government in the Economy   48

4 Models of Government   53
Government as Benevolent Social Guardian   54
Alternative Models of Government   59
Costless and Fully Informed Administrative
Capacity?   66
Conclusions   73

5 **Political Economy of Trade and Payments
Regimes**   75

6 **Political Economy of Agricultural Pricing Policies**   91
Origins of Agricultural Pricing Policies   92
Market Responses to Government Policies   96
Political Reactions   98
Questions for Political Economy   101

7 **Macroeconomic Political-Economic Interactions**   107
Sequences of Macroeconomic Political-Economic
Interactions   109
Buildup to Economic Crisis   119
What Determines Whether to Reform   124
What Determines the Nature of Reforms   129
What Determines the Success of Reforms   132?

8 **Conclusions**   135
Cycles of Policy-making   135
Is There a Political-Economic Evolution?   138

Notes   143
References   157
Index   165

List of Tables

Table 1.1 Indicators of growth and debt for developing countries   2

Table 1.2 Indicators of debt-servicing burdens   3

Table 1.3 Reform programs undertaken in the late 1980s supported by the IMF and World Bank   5

Table 2.1 High-inflation experiences in developing countries, 1964–89   16

Preface

The work that follows is an expanded version of the Ohlin Lectures that I presented to the Stockholm School of Economics in October 1990.

Bertil Ohlin was one of the intellectual giants of economics in the twentieth century. His influence on international economics, and economic policies, has been enormous. If he had confined his endeavors to the university, his contributions there would place him in the top rank of economists. However, through his own political involvement, he exemplified the ideals that many economists hold, using the tools of economics for informing good policy-making. For that reason it seemed appropriate to focus on political-economic interactions in policy making in a series of lectures in his honor.

In preparing the lectures for publication, I benefited greatly from the stimulating and lively comments and discussion in Stockholm when the lectures were presented. I am especially indebted to Mats Lundahl and Stefan Burestam-Linder for their helpful comments and suggestions. I also wish to thank Professor Lundahl and other members of the Stockholm School for their superb hospitality. My visit was not only stimulating, but it was very enjoyable. Finally, thanks are due to Gail McKinnis for her careful and efficient attention to the many details that are involved in preparing a manuscript for publication.

Political Economy of
Policy Reform in
Developing Countries

1 Introduction

For most developing countries the 1980s were a traumatic decade. After the second oil price increase in 1979, the world economy entered a recession, which was accompanied by the most severe decline in commodity prices since the 1930s, unprecedentedly high nominal and real interest rates, and the first contraction of international trade in the postwar era. Because of these, and other, events country after country was unable voluntarily to service its debt, and the worldwide "debt crisis" ensued.

The debt crisis in turn did not disappear but was transformed into an era of very slow economic growth (see table 1.1). At best, there was only moderate success in restoring growth and achieving more sustainable debt-servicing ratios (see table 1.2). However, developing countries had widely divergent experiences, as can be seen from tables 1.1 and 1.2. Some were highly successful and evidently largely immune from the international economic turmoil. They weathered the recession, terms of trade, and interest rate shocks with a slowdown in growth but were then able to resume, and even accelerate, growth and simultaneously lower debt-servicing ratios. The East Asian countries were the most prominent representatives of this group. As can be seen from table 1.1, they experienced even higher average growth rates of per capita incomes in the 1980s

Table 1.1
Indicators of growth and debt for developing countries in the 1980s

	1965–73	1973–80	1980–89
Growth rate of real GDP per capita			
All developing countries	3.9	2.5	1.6
SubSaharan Africa	2.1	0.4	−1.2
East Asia	5.3	4.9	6.2
South Asia	1.2	1.7	3.0
Europe, Middle East, North Africa	5.8	1.9	0.4
Latin America and Caribbean	3.8	2.5	−0.4

Source: World Bank, *World Development Report*, 1991, p. 3

than in the preceding decade and simultaneously were able to lower their debt–service ratios. Other countries, apparently subject to no greater external shocks, experienced continuing slow, or even negative, growth *and* were unable to reduce their debt–service burdens. The severely indebted developing countries of Latin America and SubSaharan Africa were the most visible of this group. SubSaharan Africa actually experienced declining per capita income in the 1980s, and some countries' average standards of living even fell below those prevailing at independence thirty years earlier.

These events in turn prompted a rethinking of development and development strategy. Sorting out the ways in which inappropriate economic policies had led to the difficulties of the 1980s was a major challenge and a central focus of research in development economics during the 1980s. By the end of the 1980s, a reasonable consensus had emerged as to what had gone wrong. That is, those countries that were unable to adjust and resume growth were those whose economic policies had been highly detrimental to growth. The detrimental effects of these policies had earlier been masked by the positive impact of the buoyant

Table 1.2
Indicators of debt-servicing burdens (percent)

Country group	Debt to exports				Debt service to exports			
	1980	1982	1985	1989	1980	1982	1985	1989
All developing countries	134	182	214	187	22	28	28	22
Without debt-servicing difficulties	78	96	121	86	11	15	20	14
With debt-servicing difficulties	159	232	268	272	27	36	33	29
Severely indebted								
Middle income	196	297	318	294	36	49	37	29
Low income	96	214	296	493	10	20	30	23
By region								
SubSaharan Africa	97	185	244	371	11	20	28	22
East Asia and Pacific	90	114	137	90	14	18	24	16
South Asia	161	210	265	273	12	15	23	25
Europe and Mediterranean	104	142	153	131	18	24	24	19
Middle East and North Africa	136	145	194	250	20	21	24	31
Latin America and Caribbean	197	272	315	284	37	48	39	31

Source: World Bank, *World Debt Tables 1990–91*, vol. 1, p. 20.

world economy and the ease of initial gains in output once efforts at development had begun.

As those findings became clearer, however, they raised two related sets of questions of interest to both economists and political scientists. The first set of questions centered around the process of policy reform: What had to be done? How could it be accomplished? What were the political and economic circumstances under which it could be successfully undertaken? The second set of questions focused more directly on the political and economic determinants of policy choice. Why had such inappropriate policies been adopted in the first place, and why had they been perpetuated when they were manifestly increasingly inconsistent with attaining the evident political objectives of economic growth?

Answers to these questions are of great interest for understanding the development process. However, they also have enormous and urgent practical importance. In light of the manifest failure of earlier economic policies, many countries' governments have announced economic policy reforms and reform programs.

Table 1.3 provides a listing of policy reform programs undertaken with the support of the International Monetary Fund (and often the World Bank as well) during 1987, 1988, and 1989. As such, the list does not cover countries that undertook policy reform earlier, or without Bank or Fund support. Nor does it cover support for reform efforts that took forms other than policy-based lending. It is nonetheless indicative of the extent to which policy reform efforts became the order of the day.

The programs listed in table 1.3 varied widely in objectives, in scope, and in implementation. The conditions under which these programs have been announced have differed widely. So have outcomes: Some have failed, some have met with initial success only to have the gov-

Table 1.3
Reform programs undertaken and supported by the IMF and World
Bank, 1987–89

Country	Number of loans and credits	Amount of support (millions of U.S. dollars)	Nature of loans
Algeria	2	500	1 SAL, 1 Standby
Argentina	5	3,836	3 Secals, 2 Standbys
Bangladesh	5	988	3 Secals, 2 Standbys
Benin	2	73	1 SAL, 1 SAF
Bolivia	5	450	2 Secals, 1 Standby, 1 SAF, 1 ESAF
Brazil	1	1,469	1 Standby
Burundi	4	183	1 Secal, 1 SAL, 1 Standby, 1 SAF
Cameroon	2	233	1 SAL, 1 Standby
Central African Republic	7	166	1 Secal, 3 SALs, 2 Standbys, 1 SAF
Chad	3	103	2 Secals, 1 SAF
Chile	4	1,424	2 SALs, 1 Standby, 1 EA
China	2	1,000	1 Secal, 1 Standby
Colombia	1	300	1 Secal
Congo	2	96	1 SAL, 1 Standby
Costa Rica	3	206	1 SAL, 2 Standbys
Dominica	2	7	1 SAL, 1 Standby
Ecuador	4	430	1 Secal, 3 Standbys
Egypt	1	323	1 Standby
Equatorial Guinea	2	26	1 Standby, 1 SAF
Gabon	3	221	1 SAL, 2 Standbys
The Gambia	5	76	2 SALs, 1 Standby 1 SAF, 1 ESAF
Ghana	10	1,441	3 Secals, 3 SALs, 2 Standbys, 1 SAF, 1 ESAF
Guatemala	1	72	1 Standby
Guinea	5	192	1 Secal, 1 SAL, 2 Standbys, 1 SAF
Guinea-Bissau	3	39	2 SALs, 1 SAF
Guyana	2	78	2 SALs
Haiti	2	38	1 Standby, 1 SAF
Honduras	1	50	1 SAL
Hungary	4	971	1 Secal, 1 SAL, 2 Standbys
Indonesia	2	650	1 Secal, 1 SAL

Table 1.3 (continued)

Country	Number of loans and credits	Amount of support (millions of U.S. dollars)	Nature of loans
Ivory Coast	7	865	3 Secals, 4 Standbys
Jamaica	5	474	1 Secal, 4 Standbys
Jordan	2	227	1 Secal, 1 Standby
Kenya	7	886	3 Secals, 1 Standby 2 SAFs, 1 ESAF
Korea	1	286	1 Standby
Laos, People's Democratic Republic	2	67	1 SAL, 1 SAF
Lesotho	1	15	1 SAF
Madagascar	6	353	3 Secals, 2 Standbys, 1 ESAF
Malawi	5	242	3 Secals, 1 Standby, 1 ESAF
Mali	6	207	3 Secals, 2 Standbys, 1 SAF
Mauritania	7	195	2 Secals, 1 SAL, 2 Standbys, 1 SAF, 1 ESAF
Mauritius	1	25	1 Secal
Mexico	11	9,509	9 Secals, 1 Standby, 1 EA
Morocco	6	1,419	2 Secals, 1 SAL, 3 Standbys
Mozambique	3	215	1 Secal, 1 SAL, 1 SAF
Nepal	4	163	2 SALs, 1 Standby, 1 SAF
Niger	5	181	1 Secal, 2 Standbys, 1 SAF, 1 ESAF
Nigeria	5	2,519	3 Secals, 2 Standbys
Pakistan	4	1,378	2 Secals, 1 Standby, 1 SAF
Panama	2	192	1 SAL, 1 Standby
Papua New Guinea	2	85	1 SAL, 1 Standby
Philippines	6	2,511	3 Secals, 2 Standbys, 1 EA
Poland	1	741	1 Standby
Sao Tome and Principe	3	18	2 SALs, 1 SAF
Senegal	7	504	1 Secal, 2 SALs, 2 Standbys, 1 SAF, 1 ESAF
Sierra Leone	3	231	1 Standby, 2 SAFs

Table 1.3 (continued)

Country	Number of loans and credits	Amount of support (millions of U.S. dollars)	Nature of loans
Somalia	3	153	1 Secal, 1 Standby, 1 SAF
Sri Lanka	2	303	1 SAL, 1 SAF
Tanzania	7	610	5 Secals, 1 Standby, 1 SAF
Thailand	1	408	1 Standby
Togo	6	199	1 SAL, 3 Standbys 1 SAF, 1 ESAF
Trinidad and Tobago	3	283	1 SAL, 2 Standbys
Tunisia	7	1,063	4 Secals, 1 SAL, 1 Standby, 1 EA
Turkey	5	808	5 Secals
Uganda	5	618	1 Secal, 2 SALs, 1 SAF, 1 ESAF
Uruguay	2	265	1 SAL, 1 Standby
Venezuela	5	6,145	3 Secals, 1 SAL, 1 EA
Yugoslavia	4	1,742	1 SAL, 3 Standbys
Zaire	5	845	1 SAL, 3 Standbys, 1 SAF
Zambia	1	269	1 Standby

Sources: International Monetary Fund and World Bank *Annual Reports*, 1987, 1988, 1989, and 1990. World Bank and IMF, Washington, DC.

Secal	=	sectoral adjustment loan (IBRD or IDA)
SAL	=	structural adjustment loan (IBRD or IDA)
Standby	=	IMF Standby
SAF	=	IMF Structural Adjustment Facility
ESAF	=	extended SAF
EA	=	extended arrangement

Note: Amount reflects committed support.

ernmental decision makers abandon the program, some have temporarily achieved objectives after which economic conditions reverted to the status quo ante, and some have resulted in far-reaching changes in economic and political conditions. As can be seen, there are very few developing countries that did not make at least some effort at reform.

Successful or not, most of these programs imposed short-term economic and political costs upon the decision makers who undertook them and upon many in the societies in which they were undertaken. Moreover, when programs failed, that seldom was the end of the story. New efforts at reform were often undertaken.

Improved understanding of the reform process and its essential characteristics might perhaps provide a basis on which future programs will stand a greater chance of permitting a resumption of growth in living standards in developing countries. The questions as to the policy reform process and to the political economy of economic policy determination are closely interrelated, although they are not the same. Economists have focused much of their attention on the policy reform process and developed a "political economy" of policy determination. Political scientists have also examined the politics of failed economic policies and the difficulties of reform.

It is the purpose of these lectures to address the political economy of economic policy determination and evolution in developing countries. Much has been learned, and more is being learned every day, about the interaction of economic and political variables in developing countries. Understanding of those interactions, and their evolution over time, is of interest in its own right and enriches our insights into the process of economic policy formulation and execution in all societies. In addition it is increasingly appreciated that an improved understanding is essential if economists are to be able realistically to provide technical assistance in the formulation of economic policy reform programs.

In these lectures I discuss the insights that are emerging from this line of research. In some instances there are reasonably firm conclusions; in others, the questions are at least fairly well formulated, but the answers are still in dispute. An overview of the emerging view of the political economy of economic policies in developing countries might in itself be a useful step in furthering understanding.

There are three major themes. The first two have arisen in the economics and the political science literature. The first is that politically determined policies have economic consequences that can and do change the political equilibrium that generated those policies. Market reactions to politicians' decisions influence both individual politicians and their further decisions and also change the nature of the political balance among competing political groups. Second, for many purposes, analyses of the political economy of economic policy determination in developing countries can only be undertaken on the basis of assumptions about the nature of governments. The adoption of the same economic policies in response to the same (economic) circumstances will, for example, have different consequences under a politically strong leadership of a government with a well-functioning bureaucracy capable of carrying out the wishes of the leadership than it will when a weak leadership of a coalition attempts to do the same things in circumstances where bureaucrats believe that they can generate support for opposition to those policies.

These two themes, however, imply yet a third proposition, less frequently noted in the literature to date. That is, the first two premises combined imply that it is often unsatisfactory to discuss either economic policies or governments as one-shot, enduring phenomena. The adoption by a government—be it a weak democratic coalition, a strong dictatorship, or any other type—of particular economic policies usually sets in motion political and economic responses that are likely to change both the nature of the government and the economic policies. Thus "policy cycles" of various types may emerge where neither the governmental type nor the set of economic policies are exogenous. Earlier policies and market reactions to them may determine what the political coalitions are, and what economic policies are adopted. Those policies in turn would have effects on the evolution of markets and political coalitions.

The elaboration of these themes will not be complete, since much remains to be learned. Much of what can be confidently said focuses on the political responses to economic policies and the economic consequences of alternative political decisions. Nonetheless, understanding the extent to which politicians and economic policies are endogenous, and in part dynamic, is also important.

To develop the case, background on the sorts of economic policies that have had disastrous results is essential. That is the subject of chapter 2. A next question is how such policies came about. That topic is covered in the subsequent chapter. Attention then turns to the sorts of assumptions that can be made about the nature of decision making within governments. That is covered in chapter 4. Chapter 5 then examines the political economy of agricultural pricing policies to show how policy formulation and execution interacts with both the political and the economic equilibrium. Chapter 6 is devoted to a similar analysis of trade policy. In chapter 7 the more general issue of political-economic interactions, and the cycles that can emerge from these interactions, is addressed. A final chapter then considers the question: What brings about reform? When is there an exogenous element in policy? What is the role of economists in the policy reform process?

2 Economic Policies in Developing Countries

In 1982 Mexico—an oil exporter whose export earnings had grown more rapidly over the preceding decade than almost any other country—found that it had borrowed so heavily that voluntary debt servicing could no longer be continued. A balance-of-payments crisis was taking place in a country where no one could conceivably blame the international economy. To achieve this condition, the Mexican government in 1982 had done a number of things: (1) it raised the basic wage 45 percent at the end of 1980, (2) it borrowed so heavily that the debt–export ratio was constant throughout the period of rapid growth, and (3) it planned government expenditures and revenue for 1982 to result in a fiscal deficit of 20 percent of GNP. It incurred a fiscal deficit equivalent to 17 percent of GNP despite the fact that expenditures were cut back massively starting in August of that year.[1] Perhaps even more fundamental, the Mexican government had for almost a decade rapidly increased government expenditures with little regard to their productivity. The government's share of GNP had risen from 21 percent of GNP in 1970 to 48 percent of GNP in 1982.[2] There was no question in the minds of informed Mexicans that the crisis had come about through excesses of Mexican economic policy, although it was naturally more severe because of worldwide conditions.

In January 1980 Prime Minister Süleyman Demirel announced that the government of Turkey was embarking upon a major program of economic reforms. At that time real GDP is estimated to have been declining for more than two years; inflation had reached an annual rate in excess of 100 percent; import shortages were so great that there was inadequate gasoline for the transport of coal and lignite for heating of buildings in the cold Anatolean winter, or to bring in the entire harvest, or to keep factories dependent on imports of materials operating at even 50 percent of capacity.

In Ghana, by 1984, the real return received by peasants for their cocoa when they sold it to the Cocoa Marketing Board is estimated to have been less than 33 percent of what it had been fifteen years earlier.[3] Once the preeminent exporter of cocoa in the world, Ghana had experienced declining production and export of cocoa for more than a decade. Simultaneously the annual rate of inflation was over 100 percent, and the official exchange rate was about 2 percent of the black market exchange rate. There was a chronic shortage of foreign exchange, and the economy was in perpetual crisis. Ghanaian living standards had been declining at an average annual rate of 1.6 percent since 1965. Ghana, once estimated to have a per capita income at least three times that of South Korea and Taiwan, had a per capita income estimated to be $400 per year—about 12 percent that of Korea and probably about equal to Korean per capita income in the early 1960s.

The list could continue. Peru in the late 1980s had been undergoing a rapid economic collapse, and real GNP fell more than 10 percent in 1987–88, while inflation reached an annual rate in excess of 3,500 percent a year later. Argentina's economic difficulties of the 1980s are well known, for that country had about the same living standards in

1990 as in 1965 after years of inflation, balance-of-payments crises, and large fiscal deficits. Sudan, the Philippines, Brazil, Zambia, Niger, Uganda, Bolivia, and Jamaica are among the many other countries whose sad economic deterioration could as well be documented.

While no country, developed or developing, has policies that are entirely oriented to attaining rapid economic growth, many developing countries, including those just named, had government policies that created an economic environment so inimical to growth as to cause wonderment as to why economic decline was not more precipitous. Analysis of why policies have been what they were is left to subsequent chapters. In this chapter the purpose is to note the characteristics salient for later analysis of political-economic interactions in policy formulation and execution. In attempting to understand the political economy of economic policy in developing countries, three aspects of economic policy must be considered. The first centers on the similarity in the policy stances across policies in those countries where economic performance has been poor. The second is the difference in policies between those countries and the "high flyers" among the developing countries, and the effects that those differences have had on rates of economic growth. The final aspect pertains to the apparent presence of policy cycles.

Across-the-board Economic Policy Difficulties

It will be noted later in this chapter that some countries have altered economic policies and greatly improved their economic performance. One of the interesting characteristics of economic policies in developing countries is that there appears to be a strong correlation between the types of economic policies pursued with regard to various facets of economic activity. Countries that, for example, adopt highly restrictive import licensing practices are also countries that are likely to be found having established large numbers of inefficient (in both an economic and engineering sense) parastatal enterprises, to have agricultural pricing and other policies that greatly discriminated against farmers, and to have stringent credit rationing at negative real interest rates. Those same countries that have excessive and antigrowth levels of intervention in labor and capital markets, and in major productive sectors of the economy, also generally have delivered woefully inadequate levels of infrastructure services. On one hand, countries with inappropriate economic policy frameworks typically have insisted that infrastructure services must originate in the public sector. On the other hand, road and rail networks are inadequate and generally poorly maintained; communications facilities are unreliable and in short supply; and electricity, water, and sewer services are irregular and supply only part of the population. Even education and health are neglected relative to countries whose other economic policies are more conducive to efficiency and growth.

For those of us accustomed to criticizing such poor economic policies as the U.S. fiscal deficits and the European Common Agricultural Policy, it is necessary to remind ourselves just how bad policies are. Although there are clearly interrelationships and overlaps, a convenient categorization of them would be: macroeconomic policies; trade and exchange rate policies; policies affecting agriculture; policies affecting factor markets; controls over private sector activities; economic behavior of parastatal enterprises; and the public sector expenditure program, including investment and maintenance of infrastructure. There are of course important interactions between these. Nonetheless, it facilitates exposition to discuss each separately.

Macroeconomic Instability

The instability of macroeconomic policies in developing countries is well known. Developing countries as a group averaged 49 percent average annual rate of inflation over the ten years starting in 1980.[4] Table 2.1 gives data for thirty developing countries which the International Monetary Fund terms "high-inflation countries."

As can be seen, more than twenty-five developing countries have experienced "high inflation," as classified by the Fund. These criteria are somewhat restrictive: To be classified as chronic inflation, the rate of price increase must have exceeded 20 percent for five or more years, acute inflation is deemed to have occurred when the rate has exceeded (not averaged) 80 percent for two or more years, and runaway inflation is an annual rate in excess of 200 percent for at least one year.[5] On less stringent criteria, many more developing countries would be shown to have had high rates of inflation.

Rates of inflation such as these impose large economic costs on many segments of society. Indeed, as will be seen in later chapters, a high (and generally accelerating) rate of inflation can be the impetus for political change because of the high costs to consumers and producers alike. It also generates sizable dislocations, in that economic activity is centered increasingly on short-term horizons at the expense of undertakings that might have a higher economic rate of return over a longer-term period in a more certain economic environment. Relative price changes are larger than they are under more stable price regimes and provide weaker "signals" for private economic activity, since variability of the real exchange rate, real interest rates, and relative prices of goods and factors of production may be attributable either to different timing of price increases or changes in underlying economic conditions.

Table 2.1
High-inflation experiences in developing countries, 1964–89

Country	Chronic inflation[a] Years	Annual rate (percent)	Acute inflation[b] Years	Annual rate (percent)	Runaway inflation[c] Years	Annual rate (percent)
Argentina	—	—	1975–89	281	1976	443
	—	—	—	—	1983–85	529
	—	—	—	—	1988–89	1,087
Bolivia	1967–71	23	1982–86	776	1983–86	1,133
Brazil	1974–79	39	1980–89	234	1984–85	223
	—	—	—	—	1987–89	606
Chile	—	—	1973–79	265	1973–76	329
Colombia	1973–77	24	—	—	—	—
	1985–89	24	—	—	—	—
Ecuador	1983–89	41	—	—	—	—
Ghana	1975–84	65	—	—	—	—
Guinea	1980–84	32	—	—	—	—
Guinea-Bissau	1983–89	53	—	—	—	—
Indonesia	—	—	1964–68	221	—	—
Mexico	1980–85	54	1986–88	110	—	—
Mozambique	1983–89	48	—	—	—	—
Nicaragua	1964–73	27	—	—	—	—
Paraguay	1979–84	33	—	—	—	—
	1984–89	24	—	—	—	—
Peru	1975–82	52	1983–85	127	1988–89	1,828

Sierra Leone	1981–85	51	1986–87	125	—	—
Somalia	1979–87	41	1988–89	94	—	—
Sudan	1978–89	35	—	—	—	—
Tanzania	1980–89	30	—	—	—	—
Turkey	1977–89	48	—	—	—	—
Uganda	—	—	1979–81	101	1987	256
	—	—	1985–88	166	—	—
Uruguay	1964–69	65	1967–68	106	—	—
	1971–81	60	—	—	—	—
	1983–89	65	—	—	—	—
Yugoslavia	1979–85	42	1986–89	258	1989	1,234
Zaire	1974–86	50	1986–89	84	—	—
Zambia	1984–89	46	—	—	—	—

Source: International Monetary Fund, *World Economic Outlook*, May 1990, p. 54.

Note: The IMF also listed Israel, Laos, Poland, and Vietnam as high-inflation episode countries. Those numbers are omitted here.

a. Chronic inflation is defined as annual rates of 20 to 80 percent over five or more consecutive years.

b. Acute inflation is defined as annual rates of inflation over 80 percent for two consecutive years.

c. Runaway inflation is defined as an annual rate of 200 percent or more for one year or more.

Rates of inflation, such as those reported in table 2.1, are the outcome of rapid growth of the money supply. Rapid money growth in turn is closely associated with sizable public sector deficits over long periods of time. While there is disagreement over the appropriate measure of public sector deficits, there is no question but that eventually large deficits result in high rates of inflation. In the short run, possibilities for borrowing from abroad and even domestic borrowing may permit deficits without accelerating inflation. But if over a longer period of time public sector expenditures do not generate an adequate real rate of return, mounting interest costs of servicing the debt themselves fuel increases in the deficit and raise financing requirements, which must ultimately be met by increasing the money supply.[6]

For present purposes it suffices to note that in 1982 the average public sector deficit of Latin American countries, as reported by the IMF, was 6.85 percent of GDP, while that for Africa was 6.98 percent of GDP. Some countries incurred much larger budget deficits. Mexico's 17 percent of GDP has already been mentioned. Zambia's fiscal deficit reached 21 percent of GDP in 1986 and exceeded 12 percent of GDP in every year between 1985 and 1988.[7] Moreover recorded deficits sometimes fail to capture budgetary excesses, since economic crises occur during the course of the year and annual averages reflect both the period of excess and the period of retrenchment.

To a very great degree, these deficits were fueled by the size and growth of the public sector: Mexico's central government expenditures mushroomed, as already noted; Sri Lanka's rose from 22 to 33 percent; and Kenya's rose from 23 to 30 percent.[8] Other countries already had very large public sectors: Central government expenditures as a percent of GNP in 1980 were 40 in Jamaica, 36 in Gabon, 31 in Liberia, 37 in Zambia, 30 in Tanzania, and 34 in Morocco.

Even these recorded expenditures exclude public sector enterprises, which were important in many lines of activity. Public sector enterprises, as will be discussed shortly, often incurred large "off-budget" deficits because they incurred losses that were then financed by borrowing from the central bank or other draws on public funds.

It has already been mentioned that weak delivery of infrastructure services was a hallmark of countries that tended to be highly interventionist in private economic activity. This weakness extended from unreliable telephones, power, and transport to neglect of education, health, and other social sectors. Similarly weak tax collection systems have been characteristic of many of those countries. Tax structures themselves were generally inefficient, and collected taxes were often small fractions of what those structures should have yielded.

Trade and Exchange Rate Policies

One of the best-documented cases of inappropriate economic policies and their costs is trade and exchange rate policies. For a variety of reasons discussed in chapter 3, nominal exchange rates were held constant, or adjusted only partially and after considerable delay, in the face of domestic rates of inflation considerably above the world rate and negative terms of trade shocks. When these exchange rates become increasingly overvalued, governments usually resorted to increasingly stringent import licensing in an effort to prevent unfinanceable current account deficits. Policies designed to promote domestic industry further offered across-the-board protection to domestic producers.

Real appreciation of the exchange rate during high-inflation periods led to reduced incentives for exporting, with consequent tightening of import restrictions. Since eventually the exchange rate had to be altered, the variability of the real exchange rate was high. Sebastian Edwards has calculated the coefficient of variation of the real exchange rate for thirty-three countries, based on quarterly data over the 1965–85 period. Among them, the highest variability was in Sri Lanka, with 52.5 percent, and the lowest Singapore, with 6.32 percent. The maximum real exchange rate was often a multiple of two or more times the minimum real exchange rate: In Brazil the maximum was 115 while the minimum was 50; in Chile the maximum was 148 and the minimum 19.[9]

Efforts to maintain unrealistic exchange rates through exchange controls had a number of adverse economic consequences. Black market exchange rates, with consequent over- and underinvoicing of imports and exports, were multiples of five, ten, and even fifty times the official exchange rates. In some instances smuggling of major export commodities across borders (in order to avail of the black market rate, to obtain foreign exchange, or to receive higher domestic prices in neighboring countries) resulted in erosion of official foreign exchange receipts greatly in excess of the true reduction in commodity exports. In other instances exports fell as producers shifted to alternative commodities, increased inventories in anticipation of exchange rate changes, or domestic consumption increased.

Some of the anecdotal excesses may be atypical, but they do illustrate the waste involved. In the mid-1950s import licensing in Turkey was very restrictive, since export earnings were declining and the nominal exchange rate was constant in the face of an average inflation rate in excess of 20 percent. In that environment the Turkish authorities discovered that Turkey was the largest importer of the *Times* and investigated. They discovered that as imports of cigarette paper had been prohibited, Turkish citizens had found the *Times* to be far preferable to domestic paper for rolling cigarettes. When in 1966 India devalued the rupee, it was noted that export earnings actually fell. At first it was suspected that this decline was due to "inelasticity," but investigation revealed that there had been sizable incentives for "nontraditional" exports and that faked invoicing had been taking place to obtain the subsidies.[10] More recently, when the Peruvian authorities began providing export subsidies in an effort to offset the negative incentive effects of exchange rate overvaluation, it was discovered that there had been large exports of rocks in Peru which were then dumped at sea to collect export subsidies. There are also recorded instances of "negative exports," where the import content of the export exceeded the foreign exchange received for the commodity.[11]

While exchange rate overvaluation discouraged exports and provided incentives for uneconomic behavior, protection to domestic industry was equally uneconomic. Protection equivalent to hundreds, and occasionally even thousands, of percentage points often resulted in very high cost and economically inefficient industrial activity. Not only were there very high levels of effective protection (or the equivalent in the form of import restrictions and prohibitions), but variation in rates of effective protection among economic activities was very large. In Nigeria in 1980, for example, effective protection rates ranged from minus 62 to plus 1,119 percent for 107 different manufacturing industries.[12]

Much of the protection was virtually automatic once domestic production began. This automatic protection resulted in very weak incentives for engineering or economic efficiency in private or public sector firms. On one hand, import prohibitions prevented significant competition from abroad. On the other hand, the rationing of intermediate goods imports generally and licensing of new investment ventures usually precluded the emergence of new domestic competitors and virtually guaranteed market shares for those already in the industry. Thus high-cost and low-cost firms coexisted in many industries, with very weak market pressures for expansion of the latter and contraction of the former. Overvaluation of the exchange rate, combined with preferential access to credit for new manufacturing industries, also resulted in strong incentives for the use of capital-intensive and labor-saving techniques of production. In most countries following these policies, industrial employment grew only slowly, if at all.

Policies affecting agriculture were as uneconomic as were trade and payments regimes. Overvaluation of the exchange rate suppressed the producer prices of exportables. In addition governments systematically taxed export crops heavily, both directly and through imposition of agricultural marketing boards. These boards were usually given monopsony power over the purchase of export crops and were therefore able to fix prices to be paid to farmers.

The economic consequences of marketing boards for efficient economic distribution are discussed later along with those of other parastatai enterprises. Besides those inefficiencies, the chronic shortfall of revenues usually impelled policymakers to suppress producer prices in order to guard revenues for the state. The consequence was that the prices of major export commodities at port were relatively low because of the exchange rate, and the price paid to producers was lower still because of high marketing costs and because of the decision of the government to use exportable crops as a source of tax revenue. Although producers were sometimes able to avoid some of the implicit tax by smuggling their produce out of the country, the real costs of these endeavors still lowered their returns.

For import-competing agricultural commodities there was usually some protection against imports, although the extent of currency overvaluation was a partial or total offset.

In addition to the impact of government policies on prices received by producers, government policies adversely affected farmers by raising the prices of both their consumption goods and the inputs they needed for growing their crops. Goods consumed by farmers were in part manufactured commodities, where prices were high because of the protection accorded by the trade and payments regime. Likewise intermediate inputs were often produced domestically at relatively high costs.

For food crops the situation was confounded further in many countries as efforts were made to maintain low consumer prices for these items. Except in countries where imports could be increased to provide those basic foodstuffs (e.g., in Egypt), there were inevitably pressures to reduce producer prices still further to avoid budgetary deficits.

To make matters worse, government expenditure and investment policies were heavily skewed toward industry. Thus the taxation of agriculture implicit in low producer prices was not even returned in the form of greater investment; it was instead used to finance infrastructure for high-cost manufacturing industries.

In all cases farmers—many of whom were and are among the poorer members of society who are supposed to benefit from economic development—were essentially heavily taxed to subsidize urban development.[13] As I will elaborate later, it is estimated that in many countries, small farmers' real incomes were less than half what they might have been in the absence of government interventions.

The evolution of agricultural policies in response to political and economic interactions and imperatives is analyzed in more detail in chapter 6. For present purposes it is sufficient to note that these policies were extremely detrimental to improved agricultural productivity and economic growth. Not only was agriculture taxed very heavily, it was taxed inefficiently in that waste was enormous relative to the resources gained and relative to more efficient (e.g., uniform, across-the-board taxes of agricultural commodities) possible agricultural taxation schemes.

Mining differed little from agriculture or manufacturing. In many countries, mines became state-owned parastatals, subject to economic and engineering inefficiencies. In other cases taxation of minerals was so high as to greatly discourage investment and maintenance expenditures. Parastatal enterprises also operated banks, hotels, insurance companies, and tourist resorts.

In most countries parastatal enterprises operated as highly inefficient producing entities in manufacturing, mining, and services. Their inefficient production and delivery of transport, power, and other business services also impaired the productivity of private business. As already mentioned, parastatals often held a monopoly on the distribution of fertilizers, pesticides, seeds, and other inputs into agriculture, in addition to the government's role in research and extension and in transport. In some countries parastatals were also given monopolies for the importation and even the domestic wholesale and retail distribution of key commodities.

The economic performance of manufacturing and mining parastatal enterprises has been, by and large, atrocious. In many developing countries parastatal enterprises received a very high fraction of total investible resources and proceeded to incur operating losses, sometimes not even covering depreciation charges. It does not require much sophistication in economics to know that if new investment yields zero or negative returns, it is not generating any economic growth.

India had by no means the least efficient parastatals. Yet in that country, by the late 1970s, the public sector accounted for 27 percent of total employment and 62 percent of productive capital. The public sector's share of total value added was only 29.5 percent, despite the fact that more than half of all investment for twenty-five years had been allocated to that sector. Even at domestic prices (which were distorted away from international prices to favor public sector outputs), this meant that the private sector was a far more efficient user of capital. Moreover, of the largest 25 companies in India, the 7 largest and 10 of the largest 12 were public. In many African countries the share of industrial activity undertaken by parastatals was even larger than in India.[14]

In addition to the absorption of a very high fraction of resources, parastatals also served as cost-raising entities for private enterprise. In many cases they were given favored access to imports and other inputs (including even available transport service and access to electric power), whose prices did not reflect their scarcity, to the detriment of private producers. In cases of parastatals producing intermediate goods, late deliveries and unreliable quality constituted still further difficulties for private producers.

Government organizations were established to provide "monopoly" importing services with the presumed intention of taking advantage of bargaining power consequent upon size. Instead, they found the terms on which they could buy and sell were significantly inferior to those earlier obtained by private traders. Quality standards were unenforced or unenforceable and often resulted in little more than bribery by peasants to officials who then accepted all the crop at the highest standard. Deliveries of inputs and shipments of crops were seldom on time, and collection or distribution points were sometimes so far away that peasants could not get there.

In most instances parastatal enterprises were ill-equipped to carry out their assigned functions. Stories of peasants refusing to surrender their crops because payment had been six months late the preceding year, of governments unable to gather the harvest due to lack of transport or storage facilities, of supposedly subsidized fertilizers being delivered to farmers at harvest time, and of administrative incompetence were the norm.[15]

Moreover government agencies confronted problems with which they were simply unable to cope. Problems with quality grading for agricultural commodities well illustrate the nature of the difficulties. On one hand, if no differentials in pricing were given by agricultural marketing boards to producers for their better-quality products, private markets developed to buy the better grades or producers simply failed to take the time and effort to produce superior quality. If, however, employees of marketing boards were empowered to determine the quality grades of the commodities they were purchasing, the scope for bribery and corruption increased enormously.

Thus, taking controls over the private sector and parastatal activities together, the public sector loomed large in almost every aspect of economic activity that has traditionally been regarded as the province of a market economy. It not only acted as a source of economic inefficiency in absorbing resources and in raising costs for private sector activities, but in many countries parastatal enterprises also contributed significantly to macroeconomic problems as their deficits mounted over time. By the time Turkey undertook policy reforms in 1980, parastatal enterprises alone accounted for a deficit equal to about 8 percent of GNP.[16]

To complete the dismal picture, it must be noted that policies affecting factor markets were no less deleterious to efficient resource allocation. In most countries interest rates were controlled and kept at rates below the rate of inflation, in the belief that this would encourage investment. This ignored the fact that investment was constrained by domestic savings and available foreign resources. It encouraged investment in large-scale, capital-intensive projects and thus resulted in starving the more traditional economic activities of capital for productivity improvement of the vast majority of the population. It also gave large windfall gains to those who were well enough connected to obtain official loans. It is reported, for example, that the Argentina Central Bank gave its employees credit at a nominal interest rate of 6 percent with which to purchase a home: This may explain the apparent absence of Central Bank opposition to rapid monetary expansion. Meanwhile in most countries a curb market, with much higher nominal interest rates, typically served small-scale, labor-intensive industrial activities and peasant farmers. By the late 1980s it was estimated that credit subsidies to Brazilian farmers exceeded 5 percent of GNP in value.

Labor markets too were highly regulated. In some instances minimum wages were set at very high levels relative to labor productivity. In Papua New Guinea, for example, it was estimated that the legal hourly minimum wage for unskilled factory workers in the late 1970s was four times that in the Philippines and seven times that in Indonesia. Papua New Guinean authorities, whose transport costs were also very high, were nonetheless puzzled as to why they could not attract foreign investment.

In other countries social insurance payments were high, and/or employers were expected to provide housing, education, training, and other benefits that raised labor costs to levels far above those that were consistent with full utilization of the labor force.[17] Prohibitions against dismissal of workers once they had been employed for more than six months or a year encouraged rapid turnover of unskilled labor and the use of capital-intensive techniques. Usually an "informal" sector developed not subject to labor and capital market regulations. Wages were significantly lower, and curb market interest rates significantly higher than in the "formal" sector, with consequent deleterious effects on output and income distribution.[18] Too much capital went to the formal sector and too much labor went to the informal sector, so highly different capital–labor ratios were observed within economies between the sectors.[19]

Controls over private sector activities included not only price ceilings (often not or only partially enforceable) and regulation of labor and capital markets but often extended significantly further. In India, firms were not permitted to invest without explicit government licensing. Even once the investment was approved, firms were not permitted to produce *more* than their investment license indicated. Many commodities could not be transported across state lines without licenses, and of course any needed imports could not be ordered without government approval.

The final item in this sad litany of economic policies and implementation gone astray has to do with the public sector investment and maintenance program. We all know how essential education, health, transportation, communications, and other infrastructure facilities are for development. Yet in most of the countries with pervasive controls over private sector activity, parastatal enterprises, and poor growth performance, infrastructure development was sadly neglected, poorly done, or both.[20] Showcase large-scale investments were often uneconomic; simultaneously even those investments that might have been highly productive were often not maintained. Stories of divided highways returning to jungle within a decade of completion, of telephone systems that do not work, of power failures with their attendant high costs for industrial activity, and so on, are rife. Expenditures on education often lagged, and even for those that were made, primary schooling was often neglected while higher education was expanded uneconomically.[21]

Contrasting Economic Policies of the High Flyers

Countries whose economic policies included strong discrimination against agriculture also tended to be countries with strong protection to domestic import-competing industry, countries with pervasive controls over private economic activity, and other large distortions in their economic policy framework. By contrast, countries that changed some of these policies tended to change the whole gamut of policies.

Thus in the late 1950s the authorities in Korea were practicing most of the sorts of economic policies described above. There was a sizable fiscal deficit and rapid (by the standards of the time) inflation, there were multiple exchange rates and highly restrictive import licensing (and considerable attendant corruption), there were a large number of parastatal enterprises, agricultural prices to producers were very low, labor markets were highly regulated, and credit was rationed at negative real interest rates.

Starting in 1958, a stabilization program began reducing the fiscal deficit, and the exchange rate was devalued. By 1960 greatly increased incentives for export reduced the bias of the trade regime toward import-substituting activities. By the mid-1960s the fiscal deficit had been all but eliminated, real interest rates were positive, quantitative restrictions on imports had been virtually eliminated, and controls over private sector activity had been reduced. Simultaneously the government took a series of measures that greatly improved the functioning of railroads, roads, ports, and telephones and provided an increasingly reliable supply of electric power. By the early 1970s the Korean trade regime could be said to have eliminated the bias in favor of import-competing goods; simultaneously discrimination against agriculture was replaced by discrimination in favor of agriculture.

The general trend has been for increasing liberalization of the Korean economy since the 1960s in virtually all markets. Some policies—such as agricultural prices—have been "overreversed," but virtually all have been changed. To be sure, the Korean economy has not been characterized and is not characterized by laissez-faire. But in contrast to the overcontrolled, overregulated, highly distorted economies described above, the Korean economy has been characterized by diminishing intervention in most spheres of economic activity, and the degree of distortion is considerably smaller.

It is well known that the results of these policy changes for Korea were spectacular. Taiwan, Singapore, and Hong Kong (which appears to be a truly laissez-faire economy) have also adopted very liberal policies and achieved similar economic results.

More recently other countries undertook policy reform, often with promising results. Chile, for example, achieved rapid economic growth by the latter part of the 1980s despite heavy indebtedness, a sharp drop in the price of copper, and the worldwide recession. The policy reforms had begun in 1973, and reversed virtually every aspect of earlier economic policies. While it required more than a decade before it became self-evident that growth was accelerating, and controversies remain over many aspects of Chilean politics and economics, there is little question that by the late 1980s almost all Chileans agreed that the new policies had brought great gains. Indeed in the first Chilean elections all major political parties pledged to maintain the economic policies of the politically discredited regime.

In 1980 Turkey also began a process of economic policy reform. This entailed a macroeconomic stabilization effort that did sharply reduce the losses of the State Economic Enterprises, Turkey's parastatals. That effort was only partially and temporarily successful, as increasing government expenditures on delivery of infrastructure services offset part of the reductions in State Economic Enterprise losses. But the exchange rate was sharply depreciated, quantitative restrictions on imports were removed, tariffs were greatly reduced and made much more uniform, intervention in agricultural markets was sharply diminished, interest rates became positive in real terms and credit rationing was virtually eliminated, and the labor market was liberalized. Again the results were a significant increase in the rate of economic growth, and in elections after a decade of change, all major parties stated their commitment to maintain the policy reforms and to provide macroeconomic stabilization.

For purposes of understanding the political economy of economic policy formation and evolution in developing countries, the interesting phenomena that arise from these and other cases are several. First, while there are variations from country to country in the degree of "badness" of economic policy, there seems to be a strong tendency for governments that intervene extensively in ways that are adverse to economic performance in one or more markets to intervene extensively in others. Second, the extremes of inappropriate policy have been so detrimental to economic performance that living standards have actually fallen. Third, evidence both from countries whose policies have changed and from countries whose living standards have fallen is clear enough so that there is a reasonably widespread consensus on what "better" economic policies are. Fourth, and finally, there is evidence that successful policy reforms can generate significant political support.

Economic Policy Cycles

All four of these observations raise important questions for political economy. Before attempting to address them, one last descriptive aspect of economic policies in the countries where policies are manifestly inconsistent with economic growth should be mentioned. That is, economic policies do not appear stationary, but rather they tend to cycle.

Several cycles have been identified in the literature, but two are predominant. One has been identified in countries where the cycle is centered upon rates of inflation; the other has been in countries where the cycle has centered on foreign exchange difficulties.

In the countries where cycles appear to center on inflation, the sequence generally takes the following form: At some point the rate of inflation becomes so high that the authorities deem action is called for. An anti-inflation program is announced, which typically includes domestic "austerity," coming about through cuts in planned or ongoing fiscal expenditures, increases in tax rates, increases in interest rates, and related measures. All of these policy changes are geared at slowing the inflation rate. Some of the measures are once and for all, while others may be ongoing. Once-and-for-all changes include items such as postponements of civil servants' salary increases or enforced days' holidays without pay, deferring maintenance expenditures on public works, imposition of temporary wage and price controls, temporary surcharges on imports, and temporary export taxes. Ongoing changes include the imposition of enforceable budget constraints on state enterprises, successful privatization (very rare until recently), permanent reductions in the number of public sector employees, tax reforms that raise ongoing revenues, and permanent shutting down of uneconomic investment projects.

Anti-inflation measures are often, but not always, accompanied by exchange rate and trade regime changes, although the primary motive for their imposition is the perceived high economic costs of inflation. Once started, the recorded rate of inflation generally drops sharply initially. Once it has fallen, a number of factors may bring about acceleration. On one hand, in cases where temporary measures were the primary policy instrument used to control inflation, the increase in fiscal expenditures and the erosion of price and wage controls through black markets all loosen whatever temporary fiscal restraint was achieved, and inflation once again accelerates. During the austerity period, there is a pronounced tendency for the recorded rate of economic growth to decline, while during the period of accelerating inflation, economic activity is—at least initially—more brisk. As inflation accelerates, the fiscal deficit tends to increase, further fueling inflation, until the next break in the cycle.

Where there have been repeated episodes of rapid inflation, unacceptably high rates of inflation have triggered cycles. This can be seen in table 2.1. Brazil in the 1980s provides perhaps the most extreme cases, where at least eleven anti-inflation plans were announced starting with the first Cruzado Plan in 1986. Chile, however, also cycled until at least the mid-1970s, as documented by Behrman (1975).

There are also countries in which foreign exchange difficulties have been the proximate trigger of the policy cycles. In those countries "foreign exchange shortages" prompt the authorities to limit the issuance of import licenses in increasingly restrictive fashion. While limitation may be relative to growth of the domestic economy and demand for imports or it may be absolute, the consequence is increasingly large premiums on foreign exchange licenses, rising black market premiums on exchange rates, and increasing dislocation of domestic economic activity, with a falling rate of economic growth or even a decline in the level of economic activity. At some point these distortions become so extreme as to goad the authorities into policy changes.

Often with the support of the International Monetary Fund, a program is announced and initiated in which changes in the trade and payments regime are the center-piece but in which fiscal measures are also usually included. Generally devaluations are sizable, the import regime may be liberalized, and incentives for exports are increased. The short-term consequence is almost always an improved current account balance (usually achieved partly through compression of imports associated with reduced domestic demand).

Once the current account balance improves, the cycle begins anew. The authorities relax import licensing (and often the domestic stance of fiscal policy). As they do so, expansion begins, and the demand for imports again begins rising rapidly. At first import licenses are fairly liberally granted, as the authorities underestimate import demand and overestimate future foreign exchange receipts. But as foreign exchange difficulties mount, import restrictiveness begins increasing, and the cycle repeats itself.

Inflation-induced cycles and foreign exchange-induced cycles are closely related. In Turkey, for example, a 1958 stabilization program was introduced because of balance-of-payments difficulties, although accelerating inflation at a fixed exchange rate was one of the major factors that had contributed to declining foreign exchange receipts. The second cycle was in 1970, where again foreign exchange difficulties appear to have been the major motive for policy reform. By 1980, when the third major devaluation-stabilization program was undertaken, controlling inflation and increasing foreign exchange availability appear to have both been motives.[22]

The stop-go cycle has been noted by many observers. Carlos Díaz-Alejandro, when analyzing the improved economic performance of the Colombian economy after the late 1960s, attributed much of it to Colombian success in changing policies so as to end the cycle.[23] Kaufman (1988) noted its presence in Argentina and Brazil in the 1970s and 1980s.

There are policy reform attempts that succeed and break the economic policy cycles. The nature of those reform efforts and the reasons that the decision makers undertake them, rather than the palliative measures that result in the continuation of the cycle, are key topics for later analysis. One of the interesting phenomena that informs the analysis of the political economic interactions in policy formulation is that the economic cycles, as just described, appear largely to be accompanied by political cycles, even in countries where the political structures appear at first glance to be quite different. That observation is elaborated upon in chapter 3.

3 Origins of Economic Policies

The preceding chapter contained a description of the economic policies that have characterized most developing countries in the past several decades. That characterization sufficed to demonstrate the economic inefficiencies of those policies: a first fact that must be noted in any political economy explanation. A second fact, only touched upon in chapter 2, is that in almost all the developing countries, economic policies have evolved over time.

In many instances that evolution entailed the gradual development of increasingly complex and inefficient controls, punctuated by the cycles that were discussed at the end of chapter 2. Interestingly, however, even those countries that have successfully altered their policy stances started out with the sorts of detrimental policies that still characterize many of them. It has already been mentioned that South Korea in the 1950s had the same sorts of economic policies, and the same unsatisfactory economic outcomes, that many developing countries still have today.

The policy extremes described in chapter 2 appear at first sight to be completely incomprehensible. Why, in any poor country, would the economic policymakers adopt policies so inimical to growth? And why, when the evidence is so overwhelming that the consequent economic performance is poor, are those policies not changed?

A first step in starting to answer these questions is to understand the origins of those policies in developing countries. Their origins are fairly straightforward to describe and understand and are the subject of this chapter. Once policies had been initiated, however, the political-economic interactions that resulted were fairly complex, and it is an explanation of the evolution of policy that is a challenge for political economy.

To a considerable extent, the leadership in most developing countries in the 1945–60 period was committed to achieving accelerated economic growth. The policies that were adopted were largely consistent with development thinking at that time. A natural starting point therefore is to consider the influences and ideas that underlay those policies.

It will be seen that policies initially chosen were widely regarded to be those conducive to development, although there were immediately visible shortcomings in execution. This observation in itself raises an important question as to the role of ideas and of ideology in the formulation and implementation of economic policy. In this chapter the question can only be raised, although it is a subject to which attention will revert in subsequent chapters, since it will be argued that ideas influence economic policies in three distinct ways: (1) in periods during which political leaders are acting as "benevolent social guardians" and genuinely seek (at least in some arenas) what they perceive to be the common good, (2) as a basis on which technocratic policymakers may act in emergency situations when normal political constraints are relaxed, and (3) in shifting the political costs and benefits of particular actions as ideas and ideology make them more or less acceptable to those being governed.

Any effort to understand the origins of the economic policies adopted by developing countries must start with a brief review of the conditions in which those policies were formulated—the ex-colonial legacy of many of the developing countries, the influence of the Great Depression, and the widespread view that the Soviet Union had succeeded in transforming the economy from underdeveloped to a developed one through central planning. The next factor influencing the choice of economic policies was the ideas emanating from economic thought at the time regarding development. The final set of considerations pertains to attitudes toward the role of government. Each of these is considered here in turn.

Initial Conditions under Which Economic Policy Was Formulated

Three important historical phenomena greatly influenced policymakers' thinking and choices in the immediate postwar period. These were (1) the strong nationalistic and anticolonial sentiments that naturally accompanied the attainment of independence, (2) the legacy of the Great Depression and its impact on the economies of the developing countries, and on economic thought, and (3) the experience of the Soviet Union's apparently successfully rapid industrialization under a command economy. It can be argued that these phenomena had their influence chiefly through the ideas of the time. Equally, however, it can be plausibly argued that it was the ex-colonial legacy, the scars of the Great Depression, and the belief (or desire to believe) in the Soviet Union's success that made policymakers and influential elites receptive to the sorts of ideas discussed below.

At any event there is little doubt that the ex-colonial legacy was important. Until the Second World War many of the now-developing countries were colonies of an industrialized country. That was certainly true of most of Sub-Saharan Africa and most of South and Southeast Asia. Even those countries—primarily in the Middle East and Latin America—that were earlier independent were perceived by their citizens to be "economic colonies" of the industrialized world. Raul Prebisch aptly captured the attitudes of the citizens of those countries toward their role in the international economy when he discussed the "center" (meaning essentially the OECD countries) and the "periphery," by which he meant the developing countries.[24]

Moreover until the late 1940s economic growth had seldom been pursued as a conscious objective of policy. Of course railroads, canals, ports, and other facilities had been fostered or directly built by governments to support economic activity. Those facilities certainly contributed to economic growth. But most undertakings had been decided upon, so to speak, because of their microeconomic attributes, rather than because they constituted part of an overall scheme for governmental involvement in the development process.

To be sure, a few countries, such as Turkey and the Soviet Union, had earlier chosen to pursue economic growth as a conscious and overarching objective of policy. But, in the case of Turkey, efforts had been largely pragmatic in response to changing conditions.[25] The Soviet Union was thought to have succeeded in transforming the economy from that of an underdeveloped country to that of an industrialized one through central planning. Moreover the Soviet Union was then viewed as the only country to have successfully made the transition—Japan was not then regarded as a major success.

It should be recalled that there were great similarities in the economic structures of developing countries. Although arguably living standards differed greatly between, for example, India and Colombia or Ghana, the perception of citizens of those countries was that the rich developed countries' economies were based on manufacturing, whereas those of the poor, "underdeveloped" economies were based on primary commodity production.[26] The self-view of the citizens of developing countries was that they were "hewers of wood and drawers of water." This was naturally regarded as completely unacceptable. Nationalist aspirations were therefore strongly tied to the desire for economic development. There was a strong perception that the ex-colonial powers had enforced the primary commodity-dependent status on developing countries and that thereby they had become economically stronger.[27]

While national leaders certainly wanted rising living standards to improve the lot of the poor, they were even more concerned with the nationalistic identification of industrialization with "development" and independence.[28] Moreover the international economy was suspect, since it was thought to have been the means by which the industrial countries had grown at the expense of developing countries. The suspicion that the colonial powers had "exploited" the developing countries as a means for achieving their own high living standards made international exchange perceived as a zero-sum game, with the gains accruing to the developed countries.

The desire for "development" as a way of achieving "equality" with industrialized countries was therefore a powerful political imperative.[29] That industrialization was the means to development was also taken as given. The next logical question would have been the means to be used to achieve development. Here the legacy of the Great Depression and the perception of the experience of the Soviet Union played a major role.

One possible answer to the question of means might have been to support rapid improvements in the quality and availability of health, education, and infrastructure services and to provide strong incentives for new private economic activities. However, the experience of the Great Depression had resulted in widespread suspicion of markets and their functioning in developed and developing countries alike. Memories of sharp declines in living standards associated with precipitate declines in terms of trade were still vivid.

Early Keynesianism was consistent with the view that there should be governmental responsibility for macroeconomic policy and the level of economic activity and private responsibility for resource allocation. However, the experience of the Great Depression, the belief that private markets had resulted in the "exploitation" of developing countries' natural resources, and the observation that private markets had in fact not delivered sustained development combined to make national leaders highly suspicious of markets. This view was reinforced by the perception that the Soviet Union had, through central planning, achieved "industrialization." While the experience of the Great Depression and its consequences provided a basis for rejecting markets, the apparent success of the Soviet Union in achieving economic development provided support for the view that governments could take responsibility for resource allocation in achieving development.

While economic historians debate the extent to which Russia pre–World War I had already industrialized, the view that the Soviet Union had been able to transform its economy from underdeveloped to developed was uncritically accepted throughout most of the developing countries. Although the majority of those countries did not embrace full governmental ownership and control of all means of production, they nonetheless believed that governmental guidance and indeed direction for new economic activities was essential.

Ideas Underlying Industrialization in Developing Countries[30]

The influence of these three factors was powerful in affecting the ideas even of economists as to policies that would support economic development in the postwar period. Seizing upon the desire for industrialization, and supported in part by the suspicion of the international economy, most development economists endorsed "import substitution" as a means for developing domestic industry.

From the perspective of an economic policymaker in a developing country in the early 1950s, the apparent superiority of the industrial enterprises in developed countries made it appear that new domestic industry could not conceivably compete with the already established firms in developed countries. That view in turn led naturally to advocacy of "import substitution" as the only feasible means of attaining the desired goal of industrialization.

There were essentially three basic ideas underlying the push for industrialization through import substitution in developing countries. The first of these was the infant-industry argument. The second was derived from the experience of the Great Depression, and pessimism about the possibility of developing exports of primary commodities. The third, related to the second, was Arthur Lewis's theory of surplus labor.

If there was a *logical* flaw in the argument, it was focus upon industrialization. However, as Bates (1981, p. 11) has pointed out, this was simply taken for granted:

Like all nations in the developing world, the nations of Africa seek rapid development. Their people demand larger incomes and higher standards of living. Common sense, the evidence of history, and economic doctrine all communicate a single message: that these objectives can best be secured by shifting from economies based on the production of agricultural commodities to economies based on industry and manufacturing.

To be sure, many economists recognized that there was confusion of cause and effect when emphasis was placed on pulling resources into industry: An efficient growth path would have witnessed productivity increases in agriculture and hence a release of resources for industry.[31] Nonetheless, that industrialization was necessary for modernization was generally taken for granted, and the infant-industry argument was then used as a rationale for relying upon import substitution to achieve it.[32]

As is well known, the infant-industry argument was (and is) the only generally accepted reason why temporary protection might improve global economic welfare in a world where all other markets function competitively and prices appropriately reflect marginal rates of transformation and substitution. The basic argument is that in a developing country there could be a potential new industry, already established in the rest of the world, that might have a comparative advantage in the long run. Nonetheless, it might not be established without public support because of dynamic aspects of cost reduction and externalities generated by those starting it. In these circumstances, if the long-run gains from the industry are sufficient to offset the short-term losses associated with initial encouragement to it, it could be Pareto optimal for the country and for the world as a whole to permit temporary protection (through a governmental subsidy to production or through a tariff) during the initial startup period.[33]

The theory of infant-industry protection needs little comment. *If* there are externalities associated with the presence of an economic activity, and if there are reasons to believe that the cost of the activity will fall over time,[34] it is certainly possible that it might not be privately profitable to undertake an economic activity that would be socially and presumably privately profitable in the longer term.

In the early years after the Second World War, economic policymakers in developing countries used the infant-industry argument as a rationale for imposing high levels of protection for domestic manufacturing industries. Whether it was genuinely believed that the infant-industry case was valid, or whether instead a desire for industrialization and self-sufficiency motivated these policies, is virtually irrelevant for present purposes, although it is germane to the political economy of protection: The infant-industry argument was certainly seized upon and used by those *wanting* to legitimize their case.

Because of the infant-industry argument many economists initially tended to view protection of industry in developing countries rather benignly. Acceptance of the infant-industry case for protection (via production subsidy or tariff) was virtually universal. Gottfried Haberler, who was more skeptical than most, acknowledged the case. In his Cairo lectures, in 1958, he stated that:

It is possible that the development of a particular manufacturing industry, or of manufacturing industries as a whole, will produce "external economies" . . . which eventually will make those industries able to stand up to foreign competition without protection. But since these economies are slow in coming, difficult to foresee, and often of such a nature that private enterprise cannot well appropriate them, private initiative may not be enough to ensure their realization.[35]

The second pillar of the ideas underlying the belief in import substitution concerned the expectation that earnings from exports of primary commodities could not increase. Policymakers were concerned that primary commodity prices would inexorably decline and that indeed growth might even be immiserizing.[36]

Pessimism about the future prices of primary commodities had several roots. First, the Malthusian doctrine notwithstanding, many economists pointed out that the demand for primary commodities was price inelastic. To be sure, that did not address the question of the income elasticity of demand, but it was nonetheless taken as sufficient grounds for questioning any growth prospects based on increases in primary commodity exports. Second, there was a belief that there was a long-term downward trend in primary commodity prices. Although the empirical evidence in support of this proposition was at least somewhat controversial, it was nonetheless widespread, and used to buttress the argument that future prices of primary commodities would decline.[37] Third, there was the experience with the Great Depression. The terms of trade for individual Latin American countries fell between 21 and 45 percent during that period. Prior to that, adherence had been largely to free trade and reliance upon exports of primary commodities. After the experience of the 1930s, and the difficulties most primary commodity exporters had adjusting to the lowered terms of trade, it was concluded that primary commodity exports were at best unreliable.[38]

It therefore seemed inevitable that with incomes expected to rise more rapidly than export earnings (and an anticipated income elasticity of demand for imports greater than one), there would have to be another way to meet the need for foreign exchange. There was also a widespread belief, again based in part on the experience of the Great Depression, that the developed countries would not permit rapid expansion of their imports from developing countries. It therefore seemed inevitable that there should be "import substitution" via infant industries in order to meet the increasing demand for imports.[39]

Arthur Lewis (1984), in viewing progress over several decades, put the case this way: "The case of inelastic export earnings was also opened up in the 1950s. International trade theory assumes that a country can always earn more foreign exchange by exporting more commodities or services. It is, however, logically possible for a country to have difficulty in earning more, whether because of barriers to its trade, low elasticities of supply, or low elasticities of demand for its products; . . ."[40] The argument was further buttressed by recognizing that if a country held sufficient monopoly power in trade and its supply of its exportable increased rapidly enough with growth, the consequent lower price of the commodity might completely, or more than completely, offset the increased volume of trade, resulting in "immiserizing growth." In many countries elasticity pessimism was a strong factor in buttressing the case for import-substitution industrialization.[41]

The third, and final, pillar of the intellectual support for import substitution came from Arthur Lewis's (1954) view of the labor supply in developing countries as being perfectly elastic. In Lewis's view, developing countries were poor because they saved so little, which in turn was a consequence of the low share of profits in national income. Raising the profit share in turn would require industrialization, which was thought to be possible only with protection. Conversely, if a developing country continued its pattern of primary commodity exports and manufactured imports, the inevitable consequence would be that the country's wages would remain at the subsistence level, set in the subsistence sector, and that profits would not therefore grow. A shift toward industry was therefore deemed desirable because it would permit growth of the profit share, which in turn would permit an increase in the savings rate.[42] Moreover, given the presence of "disguised unemployment," there was an implicit argument that the opportunity cost of labor was below the market wage.

The widespread acceptance of the infant-industry argument as a rationale for policy clearly illustrates the views of economists toward markets and governments at that time.

Interestingly there was apparently no questioning as to how, even if a prospective infant industry did exist, government officials might recognize it. In theory it was clear that a tariff (as second best to a production subsidy) might be warranted *if* the externality and dynamic conditions were met. The question as to how it might be ascertained ex ante whether any particular tariff would in fact conform to these conditions was not addressed. Nor was much attention given to the conditions under which the level of protection actually granted might be sufficiently high as to generate welfare losses greater than the gains attainable from the presence of the mature industry. Finally, there was no concern with the impact of protection on incentives—either to producers for cost control and quality or to the political process to prevent the emergence of vested interests for continued and often increasing levels of protection.

Role of Government in the Economy

The contrasting views of markets and governments implicit in the infant-industry notion are striking. Government officials were regarded as able to ascertain which industries would eventually be profitable and then to provide temporary incentives for their start-up. These same officials would then remove protection—presumably gradually—as the industry matured. Private entrepreneurs, by contrast, were thought to be unable to start these industries without government protection (due to externalities or other market imperfections) but to be able and willing to do so with protection. The question as to how government officials would obtain unbiased forecasts of streams of costs and benefits from self-interested entrepreneurs was not addressed.[43] Nor were questions raised concerning the incentives that would confront producers once protection was granted.

The underlying premises regarding markets and governments implicit in these policy prescriptions are obvious: There was a strong emphasis on the primacy of market imperfections. Market failures were thought to be relatively strong, while it was assumed that governments could correctly identify and perform economic functions. Virtually no attention was given to the possibility that there might be government failure.

An alternative view of markets and governments might have led to the conclusion that despite externalities and dynamic factors, the profitability of new industries would be so great that enough of them would anyway be undertaken by private entrepreneurs. On this view one could have accepted that there were certainly opportunities for new industries—that would generate positive externalities, that would have high initial costs, that learning by doing and other factors would subsequently reduce them— where nonetheless the prospective private profitability was sufficient so that it would pay entrepreneurs to bear start-up costs without government assistance. Focus would then have been on creating a climate of profitability generally, rather than on governmental determination of which industries would be the appropriate infants. Similarly it can be imagined that there might be genuine infant-industry circumstances but that government officials lacked the ability to discriminate between those circumstances and other pressures for protection: Protection for noninfants, or for that matter, continuing high levels of protection for genuine infants far beyond infancy, could clearly offset whatever gains might be achievable with an optimal degree of intervention.

The 1950s and 1960s view of the government's ability to determine which categories of infants were worthy of support, the level of support desirable, and its time path was therefore a fairly optimistic one. Simultaneously the vision

of the market was that it was unlikely to function sufficiently well to bring forth new industries that were economically warranted and needed, at a minimum, "guidance"
from economic planners. A similar emphasis on the role of
government pervaded thought about development. Following Lewis's reasoning about the inadequacy of savings,
and therefore of investment, the challenge of development
was thought to be that of increasing capital per worker.
Increasing the savings rate and allocating new investment
were regarded as appropriate roles for government.

On one hand, economic theory at that time was interpreted to mean that ownership was relatively unimportant
and that government enterprises could undertake industrial activities with no comparative disadvantage.[44] On the
other hand, it was widely believed that markets were highly
imperfect in developing countries. In part this perception
built upon Lewis's idea that labor was in surplus and over-
priced. In part, however, a "'structuralist" view of the development problem emerged in which it was widely believed
that for a variety of reasons the normal market responses
to increases and decreases in incentives were largely absent in developing countries.[45] The combination of the emphasis upon investment and the belief that governments
could establish economic parastatal enterprises resulted in
an emphasis on economic planning, through government,
to determine investment allocations for infrastructure, social services, agriculture, mining, and manufacturing.[46]

Thus the First Indian Five-Year Plan was generally viewed
as being less than an adequate one because it represented
only a "systematic collection and statement" of ongoing
public investment projects. The Second Five-Year Plan, by
contrast, was regarded as a "real" plan, since it included
investment and production targets for items as diverse as
the number of students enrolled in school, the additional
number of acres to be irrigated, and the level of investment

in and production of many items, including fertilizer, vegetable oils, bicycles, radios, textiles, steel, tractors, trucks, and automobiles.[47]

While South Asian governments were perhaps more explicit and articulate regarding their role in the economy, they were not alone in adopting this set of attitudes. Indeed many African leaders were explicitly "socialist" and focused upon industrialization through public sector activity as a means for achieving development. But whether intervention was through state ownership of major enterprises or control over private enterprises the end result was the same in most developing countries: It was expected that government officials would play a major role in determining the allocation of resources throughout much of the economy.

4   Models of Government

It was seen in chapter 3 that the initial choice of economic policies in developing countries was based on the strongly held view that when market failures occurred, there was a case for government intervention. Implicitly the logic of that conclusion was founded upon the twin premises that (1) a government's objective would be to achieve an economically efficient outcome (including economic growth) and (2) there would be no information costs, administrative difficulties, or other barriers to identifying and implementing policy toward those ends.

To a considerable degree, it has been the experience in developing countries that has led economists and others to question each of these assumptions. Evidence that economic policies were not consistent with economic efficiency and growth led to short-term adjustment and the policy cycles already described, but it did not lead to their alteration. That in turn raised questions as to whether the benevolent social guardian formulation of the objectives of those in government was appropriate. Simultaneously difficulties in carrying out policies raised serious questions about the second assumption. These difficulties in many cases resulted in serious political problems for political leaders, and as such were clearly unintended. Thus there was a reexamination of the premise that governmental agencies could efficiently carry out any particular tasks they were assigned.

In this chapter the questions that have been raised regarding the implicit premises are discussed, and alternative views of governmental behavior and administrative capability are critically examined. First, the benevolent social guardian model of governmental objectives and decision making is set forth and scrutinized. Then alternative models of decision making within the government are set up. Finally, questions surrounding the costless efficiency with which policy may be carried out are analyzed.

It may be noted at the outset that many of the issues addressed here have also arisen in developed countries. The difference is perhaps one of degree, but in fact the problems in developing countries were far more severe. First, the pervasive microeconomic intervention in developing countries went far beyond that in most developed countries. Second, the administrative capacity in many developing countries was far less than in the developed countries. Third, by definition, the developing countries were poorer and could less well afford the waste.

Government as Benevolent Social Guardian

The economic analysis underlying the policy prescriptions for infant industry, for indifference between market and socialist solutions (if not preference for the latter), and for governmental leadership in the quest for development had as its basis the assumption that there would be a public entity committed to achieving the common good. It was assumed that "the government" would, in the Benthamite tradition, behave as a benevolent social guardian, directing resources and activities to achieve a perfectly functioning competitive market economy and a desirable rate of economic growth.[48]

To analyze the "government as benevolent social guardian" premise, it is useful to assume for the present that whatever is decided upon by way of government policy will in fact costlessly be carried out. Thus, for discussion, the second premise underlying earlier policy analysis is—temporarily—maintained. It is critically examined later in this chapter.

The view of a benevolent social guardian state had a long tradition in economics, and in much discussion of public policy. The underlying premise was that governments and civil servants in some sense were "above the system." It/they would selflessly seek the welfare of the people, even when the people themselves did not know what was in their self-interest, and would unerringly and effortlessly know how to achieve their best interests. Hence, so the reasoning went, if there were an externality, no matter the size, there was a case for government intervention so that private individuals would appropriately perceive the social trade-off.

One argument for government intervention in developing countries, for example, was that poor people usually had too high a rate of time preference and thus gave inadequate weight to the welfare of future generations and saved too little. By contrast, it was assumed that government officials would take the welfare of future generations more into account than would private citizens and thus have a lower rate of time preference. It was thought to follow that they would, and should, therefore raise taxes for the purpose of increasing the national savings rate. Public savings were deemed desirable to offset the myopia of private citizens. This notion underlay, inter alia, the formulation of the influential Indian Five-Year Plans. In fact it has repeatedly been demonstrated that politicians are, if anything, more myopic than private citizens, and they normally have a higher rate of time preference. The negative savings of public enterprises in India have been a major source of difficulty in that country, as noted earlier.

Take another example. It was noted that in almost all developing countries, rural moneylenders charged high rates of interest to rural tenant farmers and small peasants. Deeming that this reflected a market imperfection, agricultural credit institutions were established in many countries to correct that presumed market failure by offering credit to small farmers at low rates of interest.[49]

More generally welfare economics was long based on the premise that when there were departures from a competitive Pareto optimum, there was a self-evident case for government intervention. This naturally implied that the objective of economic policy was to achieve a Pareto optimum, which in turn was based on the implicit assumption that government intervention in the economy would occur when and only when that intervention would correct market failures.[50]

If the objective of policy was to achieve a Pareto optimum, questions regarding governments' capacities to implement alternative programs and activities would still have arisen and are addressed later. In fact the benevolent social guardian view of government has itself come under scrutiny from a variety of perspectives and for a number of reasons.

First, economic theory has long been based on the premise that most individuals are pursuing their own self-interest in the private sector. That premise has been accepted as a reasonable approximation to reality, and most analyses and empirical observation of private sector economic activity and behavior are consistent with it. Few question the importance of incentives, and individual rewards and penalties, in affecting individual behavior.

Given the consistency of the assumption of self-interest with observed behavior in private economic activity, a first logical question and criticism of the benevolent social guardian rationale for policy prescription is why it should be assumed that those in the public sector will not also seek their own self-interest. After all, civil servants are interested in pursuing their careers and in economic gains. While some may be selflessly pursuing the public good, there are others who are attempting to do so while simultaneously concerned about their own careers and economic well-being. Thus, for example, civil servants will generally be loathe to recommend the elimination of their agency and will have a natural bias toward expanding the scope of their agency's activity. It is probably nothing more than human nature for most people, including civil servants, to overestimate the importance of their work contrasted with that of others.

Second, in most countries, lobbies and interest groups are widely perceived to use their influence to bring about policy outcomes they desire. These outcomes are often inconsistent with an efficient allocation of resources, although it has been argued that the political process will usually find least-cost ways of effecting the politically mandated transfers. Becker (1983), for example, has developed a model in which various groups in society spend resources on political activity in an effort to transfer resources to themselves or to prevent transfers from themselves to other groups. In his model, however, transfers are always effected in economically efficient ways so that the deadweight losses associated with the transfers (as contrasted with the resources used in the political process) are minimized.[51]

Third, it has been widely noted that in collective decision making, there can be substantial free-rider problems.[52] When many individuals stand to gain from a particular policy, each of them may view the likelihood of gain as being largely independent of his or her behavior, since each contribution to a lobby or pressure group will be small relative to the total. By contrast, when a small number stand to gain, they are more likely to perceive their own contribution as mattering, while simultaneously monitoring by other members of the group is more feasible.

Fourth, when government institutions implement controls attempting to prevent private individuals from carrying out profitable transactions or from conveying valuable property rights without charging for them, there are bound to be incentives for people to profit from receiving the property rights or to capture the profits legally or extralegally at some cost. These activities are "rent seeking" in the sense that the resources devoted to obtaining the item of value do not create value and constitute a deadweight cost.

The fact that rent seeking will normally arise in response to government controls over economic activity has a number of consequences, some of which affect the behavior of the government and some of which affect the administrative costs of implementing policies. Once valuable rights have been created by government controls, and individuals and bureaucrats are engaged in seeking and dispensing those rights and have invested resources in developing channels to obtain government favors, there exist strong interests within the government (and among the private rent seekers) for perpetuating, if not intensifying, the controls that generate the rents. There are a number of policies that can create pressures within the government to maintain the private income streams generated by controls. Hence, if there were an economically neutral policy with net costs that are precisely the costs of rent seeking for the profits inherent in controls, there would be a group within society in favor of perpetuating those controls.[53] If, otherwise, the body politic were indifferent between the maintenance and removal of those controls (e.g., because of the free-rider problem), the existence of interest groups in society seeking to protect their private earnings stream would tip the political balance in favor of perpetuating controls. Clearly, once that point is recognized, there could be a weak coalition (or majority) in favor of control removal in the absence of the rent seekers, but the marginal weight of the rent seekers could perpetuate controls.

A final line of criticism of the benevolent social guardian model of government has focused on the inherent uncertainties and informational asymmetries in economic activity. This approach goes back to the Hayekian view that the essence of economic activity is the information held only by individuals who will not be willing to reveal it to others. In this view government officials may be in a poorer position than private agents with respect to information. Informational asymmetries can prevent behavior of the sort assumed by the benevolent social guardian model. This criticism is closely linked to the problem of implementation and is therefore discussed further in the next section.

Alternative Models of Government

As experience mounted in developing countries, it became increasingly evident that governmental behavior is far more complex than that assumed in the benevolent social guardian model of the state. In response a variety of alternative assumptions about public sector decision making (and policy execution) have been suggested.

Deepak Lal and Hla Myint (1990) have suggested a topology of such models. These include models in which the state is "autonomous," pursuing objectives of its own, and models in which the state is "factional," reflecting collective decision making subject to a variety of constraints. There are several posited types of autonomous and factional states. Each type is assumed to be pursuing certain objectives. The point is not, however, that the ruler(s) or decision makers necessarily consciously pursue the objectives suggested by Lal and Myint. Rather, it is suggested that the government behaves in ways that would be observed if the objectives of policy were as indicated.

A first lesson for economists from the political science literature is that a government is not a single, rational, decision maker. Indeed use of the word "government," followed by a singular purposive verb, is normally misleading. There are always a number of influences on decisions, and they may be more or less important depending on the issue or issues at hand. To suggest that a dictator, for example, has no political constraints is highly misleading: even in dictatorships there must be groups supporting, or at least not actively opposing, the dictator. For that reason choices of certain policies will in normal circumstances be politically too costly if they seriously undermine support of key groups.

In introducing these prototypes, the notion is to characterize certain polar types of governments with quite different behavior. The questions asked may be how governments with particular objective functions would behave, and how the predicted behavior would compare with that observed in particular countries at given times.

Lal and Myint introduced their prototypes in an effort to ascertain whether certain sorts of economic situations were more conducive to some types of governmental behavior than to others. They were, for example, contrasting the political process in land-abundant countries such as Brazil with that in resource-poor countries such as Korea. In that sense their purpose was to analyze the ways in which economic constraints affect political structure.

Here the purpose is somewhat different. It will later be argued that there are complex interactions between the objectives of different types of governments, the policies pursued, and the effects of those economic policies on the political process itself. Although these interactions may be complex and not well understood, their existence should be recognized in the course of economic policy analysis. It is useful to start by characterizing the various types of state as if such states were enduring, stable entities. In chapter 5 the sorts of mechanisms that result in political-economic interactions and the transformation of states from one type to another are analyzed.

An autonomous state is characterized by Lal and Myint as one in which those in power are sufficiently entrenched so that within a fairly wide range they may pursue their objectives without paying very much regard to any political opposition to the policies undertaken. Lal and Myint subdivide autonomous states into the guardian state and two types of predatory states. The first type of predator is absolutist, while the second is "bureaucratic authoritarian."

The guardian state may be a benevolent social guardian, of the type assumed in much of the theory of economic policy. President Chung Hee Park in Korea and President Suharto of Indonesia appear to have had the economic welfare of their people sufficiently high among their objectives. They also appear to have had sufficient political power to be able to insulate much of economic policy formulation and execution from other forces—so as to have been characterizable, at least in part, as having headed governments that behaved as if they were benevolent social guardians. A strong case can be made that in many countries immediately after independence the leaders had the well-being of their people at heart and wanted to be benevolent social guardians. This certainly appears to have been the case with Jawaharlal Nehru in India and Kemal Atatürk in Turkey.[54]

However, the guardian state may also be one in which a dictator has an agenda, believed to be in the peoples' best interest but quite different from that:

The autonomous Guardian may not necessarily be benevolent in the rationalist sense of the economist or Plato. This type of State would also cover those "heroic" supermen, the proclaimed Nietzchian Guardian, "who tramples down opposition, despises happiness, and creates his own rules." Hitler, Mussolini and others of that ilk would also fall into this category of the "Guardian" state.[55]

The predatory state, by contrast, is one in which those in power are viewed as "predators," who are only marginally concerned with the welfare of their citizens except insofar as that permits a greater gain for those who are governing.[56] The predator seeks the maximum continuing flow of resources (which can include power, military aggrandizement, or other items in addition to wealth and income); in the predatory state the government will undertake investments in infrastructure and other items that increase the productivity of private factors of production but only to increase the revenues of the state as real incomes. Therefore tax revenues rise. Lal and Myint contrast the guardian state and the predatory state as follows:

One way of characterizing the difference between the Platonic and Predatory States is that individuals in charge of the instruments of power in the Platonic state have citizen's welfare in their own objective function, whilst in the Predatory State, the rulers treat their citizen's welfare more as a constraint which restricts their pursuit of other objectives. In other words, citizen's welfare is an instrument rather than an objective in the hands of the rulers in the Predatory State.[57]

In the Lal-Myint characterization, predatory states are of two basic types. The first is a state run by a single ruler: The ruler might be an absolute monarch, a colonial government in a colony, a charismatic leader, or a dictator. In this case the objective of the ruler is net revenue maximization.[58] The second type of predatory state is what Lal and Myint call the "bureaucratic-authoritarian" state, in which the objective is to maximize the number of bureaucrats, or public employment. These states are often one-party states, where maximization of public employment is a means through which the ruling party can attempt to maintain support. Lal and Myint regard most of the formerly communist states of Eastern Europe as also having been of this type.

It should be reiterated that this characterization of governmental type does not imply that the country's ruler or rulers in fact intend to maximize public employment. Rather, their policies and behavior can be interpreted *as if* this were their objective. In fact the objective might well be simply to maintain power, and increasing public employment could be perceived as the most effective way to do so.

Argentina appears to have been a bureaucratic-authoritarian factional state in most of the period from Juan Peron's presidency until the late 1980s. It is reported, for example, that Rioja, the state of which Carlos Menem was governor before he was elected president of the republic, had 40,000 state employees out of a total labor force of 100,000.

To maximize the present value of net revenue to the state from those excluded from the government, the predatory state—whether authoritarian or bureaucratic—will invest in public goods such as roads and will provide some property rights in order to increase gross output of the economy. Findlay and Wilson (1987) have formalized the model of a predatory state. In their model the "leviathan" state maximizes the "surplus" that it may seize. To do this, investments are made in public goods that increase the private sector's productivity. However, the surplus is entirely absorbed by public sector employment, and government expenditures exceed the social optimum. The welfare of those excluded from the Leviathan's concern is clearly less than it would be were the state a benevolent social guardian.[59] Findlay (1988) has argued that many Latin American governments were characterized by

a faceless junta . . . at the apex of the pyramid, exercising power through, and in the interest of, the military and civilian bureaucracy itself . . . The self-imposed tasks of the regime are "national security," with its concomitant of "internal order," and "development," which serves both as an end in itself and, if successful, as a means to further expansion of the role of the state, and therefore, of the bureaucracy itself. The Parkinson-Niskanen model of departmental or corporate bureaucracy can be applied to the state as a whole to produce the concept of a particular type of "leviathan," a Frankenstein monster in which the entities such as army and civil service, ostensibly created to serve the "peoples' will," instead arrogate to themselves the task of defining the goals of the state, which they make to coincide with their own.[60]

Autonomous states are all characterized by a relative freedom from overriding influences of particular economic interest groups. The ruler or rulers enjoy a considerable degree of freedom from direct pressure, at least in the short run. Rulers are constrained, however, in several ways. First, there is an economic constraint in that public sector revenues (which may be being maximized) are finite and thus constrain expenditures (on the army, on palaces, and on public works that may increase future revenues). Second, even rulers of autonomous states must maintain power, which may constrain the extent to which they are willing to tax or to alienate their citizens or at least particular groups of citizens. Third, there are a variety of ways in which those governed within the autonomous state can attempt to avoid the taxation and extraction of revenue of the rulers. To the extent that private citizens can avoid the predatory powers of the state, the authority of the state is undermined, and the capacity of the rulers to raise revenues diminishes. This is one of the factors that contributes to the dynamic economic-political interactions discussed in chapter 5.

The factional state, by contrast, is characterized by a coalition of different (usually economic) interest groups. There are interest groups, usually identified with separate voting and economic interests, in the body politic, and some sort of coalition is necessary to maintain the government in power. Because of this those in power in the factional state have far less autonomy—and are far more constrained in their actions—than are those governing in predatory or benevolent guardian states. The governing coalition is then seeking to maximize the well-being of the members of the coalition, subject to attempting to stay in power and the governmental budget constraint.

The factional state can be democratic, or it can be authoritarian. When it is democratic, a coalition of interests must maintain power, and resources are allocated to buying support of different members of the coalition. The factional state is much weaker—and the coalition much more fragile—than in the authoritarian state. For that reason opportunity for predation is less. Malaysia, for example, seems to be a good example of a factional state where economic policy is formulated largely in the context of a government whose objective comes close to maximizing the welfare of its Malay citizens who are mostly rice farmers and rural: Wealthy Chinese traders and entrepreneurs are the primary object of predation in that case.

When it is authoritarian, the factional state is seeking the interests of those in the ruling coalition. Bates notes that in Ghana, Kwame Nkrumah's coalition excluded all significant rural interests and governed with little regard to their well-being. By contrast, in Kenya, the ruling coalition had strong ties with rural interests, and agriculture fared much better.[61]

The factional state, especially when it is democratic, may be quite weak. Such was the case in Turkey in the late 1970s, for example, when no political party had a majority and each major party was dependent upon the support of small extremist parties if it was to form a government. The result was a coalition, whose leadership was virtually incapable of action. Formulation of any program was an impossibility for a period of several years when there were severe economic problems that would have been addressed much earlier had there been a majority government.[62]

When the state behaves as if its objective is to maximize public sector employment, or to increase its international stature through "showcase" projects, it is small wonder that economic policies are pursued that are not always consonant with Pareto optimality and economic efficiency. Likewise, when a government is evidently maximizing the resources available to "national defense," it is unlikely to be seeking welfare-maximizing economic policies with regard to agricultural pricing or the trade regime.

All that has been done to this point is to establish some prototypes of governmental behavior. How these prototypes come about, and how the economic effects of their behavior affects them, is a major concern of these lectures. Before turning to those issues, however, there remains the question of "administrative capacity."

Costless and Fully Informed Administrative Capacity?

It was earlier stated that the highly interventionist policies advocated by most policymakers and economists concerned with development were based on the twin assumptions that governments' objectives would be to behave as benevolent social guardians and that governments could achieve those objectives costlessly, or at least at very low cost. Reasons why the benevolent social guardian assumption has been challenged have already been set forth. Here the purpose is to examine the experience with "omniscient," "costless" governmental policies. For convenience it will be simplest to assume here that the objectives of policy makers are in fact those of a social guardian, and consistent with *attempting* to achieve an economically efficient solution.

Three sets of difficulties may be identified even when intentions are appropriate. First, establishing bureaucratic machinery and mechanisms that will be able to carry out desired policies is not as simple as had been assumed. Second, incentives and mechanisms are weak or lacking to induce public entities to achieve least-cost outcomes. Third, because many of the policies that were undertaken in effect were designed to prevent the carrying out of privately profitable transactions (or created valuable property rights for some), private individuals and firms often had incentives to falsify or conceal information, thus creating problems of incentive incompatibility.

Each of these sets of reasons had important economic and political consequences and therefore must be understood. Many of the factors discussed here were important factors in the political-economic interactions that are the subject of the next chapter. In many instances it was the private sectors' reactions to the shifting opportunities for profit inherent in government controls that then led to outcomes other than those evidently anticipated by policymakers. Unsatisfactory outcomes in turn not only led the existing government to attempt to alter policies but also often shifted the political equilibrium in ways that further fed into policy changes.

Consideration of those interactions cannot be undertaken until the difficulties inherent in policy implementation are examined. An appropriate starting point is the problem of establishing and then carrying out policies. A first, though seldom-noted, proposition is that different types of economic policies require differing degrees and types of implementation. A devaluation of the currency, for example, can normally be undertaken by the central bank and must be done with as little previous public discussion as possible. While complementary measures may require political and bureaucratic resources, a decision to devalue the currency can be implemented with little administrative difficulty. There may be *political* difficulties with the decision, but an alteration in the exchange rate is simple.

By contrast, deciding, for example, to distribute free fertilizer to small farmers is inherently more difficult. Clearly, if fertilizer is to be free, there must be a mechanism for deciding on each individual's entitlement, unless supplies are much greater than in any developing country yet encountered. There must also be equipment available to transport fertilizer from its origin (either port or a domestic factory) to wholesale distribution points and then a means for the retail distribution of the fertilizer. If the fertilizer is imported, the quantity to be distributed must be anticipated and ordered by an individual or group; if it is to be produced domestically, arrangements should be made for its timely availability.

In practice each of these steps can result in major dislocations. Individual bureaucrats entrusted with deciding on individual smallholders' entitlements will need information on which to base their decisions (e.g., number of hectares cultivated, possibly by crop type). If judgment is permitted, there will be opportunity for bribery of officials to obtain larger allotments; if no judgment is permitted, there will still be problems if the total supply made available for the responsible official's district is less than the sum of the entitlements under the program. Once supplies are inadequate, there is clearly opportunity for favoritism among recipients; fertilizer at the right time is worth a great deal more than fertilizer too late in the crop cycle, so timely provision at subsidized prices is clearly valuable.

Moreover fertilizer—while more homogeneous than some commodities—is not all the same. Nitrogen, potassium, and phosphate fertilizers are optimally used in different combinations depending on soil types and crops. Delivery of the wrong mix can result in serious reductions in yield, and yet delivery of the right mix requires more judgments of individual officials as to how much of which type each peasant should receive.

Officials can only distribute what they have in each locality. Arranging transport of fertilizer to these localities is therefore an important component of the delivery system. Yet in countries in which transport facilities are themselves in short supply, or where there is inadequate maintenance of trucks so that breakdowns are frequent and delivery times uncertain, local officials may not even receive fertilizer until too late in the cycle.[63]

In addition to inefficiencies generated by late fertilizer delivery, there appears to have been a pronounced tendency for larger landowners to receive disproportionate shares of subsidized fertilizer, as well as other subsidized inputs. In part this probably reflects the greater ability of wealthier farmers to assert their rights. It is also probably partly a reflection of the greater political influence of large landowners. However, a bureaucrat's life is surely easier when he must make fewer allocations than when he must make more: For that reason one might expect that areas and farms with large entitlements would be preferentially treated and thus, if total supplies were less than demand at the subsidized price, receive a disproportionately large allocation.

Fertilizer marketing was only one of many functions governments attempted to assume in many developing countries. Reasons for inefficiencies in the distribution system were many, and they extend well beyond the technical requirements of timely delivery and appropriate mix of fertilizers. But even without other complications those requirements were often inconsistent with the capabilities of the enterprises established to carry out the distribution functions.

When it came to marketing the crop, difficulties were even greater. Consider, for example, the problem of quality grading. There were two possibilities: Either there would be insufficient allowance for quality differentials, or individual employees of the marketing board would have to be empowered to pay differentially for different qualities of the product. When there was no premium for better quality, the results were immediately obvious in a lower average quality delivered to the buyers, as farmers withheld their top quality product to be marketed through alternative (legal or illegal) channels. On the other hand, when quality differentials were provided for, officials were susceptible to "influence" in ascertaining the quality of the product. Tobacco procurement in Turkey, for example, was subject to systematic misgrading. The true quality of Turkish tobacco exported, as reflected in international grading standards, declined substantially. Simultaneously, however, the average grade reported in Turkey rose. Olgun (1991, p. 260) reports that tobacco procurement personnel, who were politically well organized, often "overgraded deliveries in return for material favors." Interestingly the average grade for nationwide entrance examinations to different fields of endeavor was higher for tobacco inspectors than for any other group of high school graduates.[64]

Problems such as these surfaced in many parastatal enterprises and other government agencies in most developing countries. Politicians and bureaucrats simply failed to reckon with the technical requirements of production and distribution systems,[65] quite aside from the problems that arose with respect to quality grading, estimating the relevant levels of demand, and providing services in timely fashion.

Simple technical problems of administration also arose in a variety of other contexts. Billing of individuals for their use of electricity, for example, is infeasible in the absence of electric meters.[66] Lack of competent technicians able to diagnose and repair equipment resulted in downtime, and in an inability to determine what needed repair and what replacement.

If administrative difficulties themselves caused problems, there were few incentives for government officials carrying out economic functions to seek high levels of economic efficiency. Most parastatals—including agricultural marketing boards, transport agencies, electricity generating enterprises, and manufacturing entities—were accorded monopoly or quasi-monopoly power. Top officers were usually either politicians or civil servants with little prior experience in the relevant line of economic activity. There was usually more reward for expanding the number of new employees than for increasing productivity; indeed, if increased productivity had resulted in a potential for reducing the number of employees, most of the top officials in the parastatal enterprises involved would have been penalized, not rewarded. In fact, politically, the opposite was more likely to be true: Those managers who expanded employment significantly were more often than not the more successful.[67]

The third factor that made administration far from automatic was the informational asymmetry and incentive incompatibility of the tasks civil servants were asked to undertake and the maximizing motives of private sector actors. When applying for a foreign exchange license for new investment, for example, the private applicant had every motivation to overstate his "need" for foreign exchange, as exchange rates were typically overvalued, and there were low duties, if any, on imports of capital goods. Government officials therefore pored over blueprints of factories to attempt to ensure that "unnecessary" imports were not imported under the umbrella of the investment project.[68] It was thus not enough to decide, by whatever criteria, that an application for investment in a fertilizer factory should be approved. Given incentives, it was necessary to attempt to ensure that the items cleared under the approval were only those necessary for the "legitimate" project.

To be sure, these problems made the task of administration doubly difficult. On one hand, there was the problem of checking to make sure that private parties did not overstate their "requirements" for their approved activities. On the other hand, the authorities also had to check on shipments to see that they conformed with prior specifications. In India, for example, manufacturers of small tractors were no longer permitted to import engines once a domestic factory had been established and the entrepreneur claimed competence in their production. In fact domestically built engines were high cost and low quality. Domestic producers of small tractors therefore began importing large tractors and reselling them in the market. After this practice had been proceeding for some time, a customs inspector discovered that the tractors had an "extra" small engine. Small tractor manufacturers had imported these and saved considerably on their costs of production while improving the quality of their product. Needless to say, once the extra engines were discovered, inspection of imports was even more detailed, and delays in customs were even greater than they had been earlier.

In this instance the administrative complexities were associated with scrutinizing private sector behavior in order to ensure compliance with regulations. In other instances, of course, the administrative mandate was to establish mechanisms for preventing illegal activities such as smuggling. As with other governmental entities, problems immediately arose: How does one hire customs inspectors who will be immune to the blandishments of private individuals who stand to gain a great deal if the inspector looks the other way? In an effort to get around this particular problem, some countries have finally resorted to hiring foreign firms to undertake customs inspection.

Conclusions

All of the phenomena discussed in this chapter have impinged on the operation of economic policies in developing countries. Political decision-making bodies have by no means been as committed to the "common good," as Jeremy Bentham optimistically assumed in the nineteenth century. Simultaneously a large number of administrative difficulties arise in the course of carrying out economic activities within the public sector. Some are purely administrative; others are bound up with the incentives private individuals have to influence officials' behavior.

All of these factors, however, led to a number of "surprises," or at least unanticipated outcomes, when the policies discussed in chapter 2 were undertaken in developing countries. Those surprises in turn had consequences for the political decision-making process in the form of changed economic policies with still further repercussions. Those interactions are still only beginning to be understood, and they should be at the heart of political economy insofar as it relates to the analysis of economic policies in developing countries. To them we now turn.

5   Political Economy of Trade and Payments Regimes

No market, or sector, of the economy is more revealing with respect to political-economic interactions than the foreign trade and exchange rate regime.[69] A starting point is to note the political origins of economic policies and the market response to those policies. From there the political responses to the market and the economic consequences of those reactions can be examined.

It will be recalled that all developing countries relied heavily on imports for most manufactured commodities in the early postwar years. The initial desire to raise the rate of capital formation and to accelerate the rate of industrialization resulted in policies to protect domestic industries from foreign competition under the aegis of the infant-industry argument. In the political arena an overarching framework for economic policy was decided upon. Its ingredients consisted of a strong urge for industrialization (buttressed by the infant-industry argument), a suspicion of markets, and the belief that the government should play a central role. It was perceived that savings rates were low and that a key objective of policy should be to raise the rate of investment.

Based partly on the infant-industry argument, and partly on the premise that "balanced growth" and a "big push" were necessary in order to generate sufficiently large domestic markets to enable a satisfactory payoff on investments,[70] almost all developing countries' governments took steps to encourage "import substitution" early after attaining independence. These steps included both a legal framework to protect private import-substituting industry and the establishment of public sector parastatal enterprises. While the precise mix of reliance on private sector and development of public sector activities differed from country to country, there were few in which there was not some of each. Most African countries relied heavily on parastatals for manufacturing production. Many other countries, including Turkey and India, declared that they had a "mixed" economy, but a very large fraction of investment in manufacturing was directed toward government-owned manufacturing enterprises.

To encourage private firms to engage in import substitution, many countries made legal provisions that automatically, or quasi automatically, increased protection to private producers once domestic production had started. Thus, for example, the Brazilian tariff code had a provision that any listed tariff was to be doubled if imports were deemed to compete with domestic capacity. Further to encourage domestic industry, a "Law of Similars" was enacted, under which firms that chose to import when similar domestic goods were available lost all their privileges (including subsidized credit and the right to compete for government contracts). The combination of these measures virtually ensured prohibitive protection for newly started domestic private industries.[71]

In India and Turkey import licenses were required for importing any commodity; as a matter of policy none were granted for commodities that could be produced domestically. In India this went so far that a would-be importer had to have letters from any potential domestic supplier stating that they could not meet his order. Naturally issues of quality comparability, timeliness of delivery, and after-service vanished when domestic producers assured government officials that they could produce the product.

The initial decisions to encourage import substitution therefore were undertaken by leadership of governments, many of which were acting in their role as benevolent guardians at least regarding infant industries. Economic theory at the time embraced a similar view of government, and the policies that were adopted were regarded as consistent with economic theory.

Because it was recognized that the establishment of import substitution activities would require considerable investment with a high import content, governments were anxious to encourage investment in them and simultaneously to increasing their own expenditures "to provide the necessary infrastructure." To encourage investment, country after country developed a tariff structure in which duties and other charges on imports of capital goods were very low. Simultaneously politicians were anxious to maintain a fixed nominal exchange rate, in part to make investment more attractive and in part for "nationalistic" reasons.

While nominal exchange rates were held constant, however, increases in government expenditures almost always exceeded increases in tax revenues, rationalized by the urgent and pressing needs for economic development. The natural consequence was that inflationary pressures resulted. To be sure, the inflations in most developing countries in the 1950s and 1960s appeared small by current world standards, but it must be recalled that the world price level was virtually stable and almost all developing countries subscribed to the IMF Articles of Agreement and had fixed nominal exchange rates.[72]

There was consequently a strong tendency for real exchange rates to become more and more overvalued relative to the rate of exchange that would have been consistent with achieving a current account balance financeable by receipts from foreign aid and foreign investment. In Turkey, for example, the official exchange rate from 1953 to 1957 is estimated to have appreciated in real terms by 47 percent. Even after making allowances for increased surcharges and taxes and for export subsidies, the real return to exporters per dollar of traditional exports fell 44 percent in four years, that for nontraditional exports fell 32 percent, and that for consumer goods imports by 29 percent.[73]

In other countries, similar real appreciations of the real exchange rate occurred. Ghana perhaps had the most extreme case: By 1984 the official price of foreign exchange was about 2 percent of the black market price. When that country began its economic reform program, the number of credits per U.S. dollar was increased from 60 in 1985 to 303 in 1988.[74]

These real exchange rate appreciations had important, but unanticipated, economic consequences. The initial economic consequence was that export earnings generally increased less than anticipated, while the demand for imports rose sharply. In some countries, especially former British colonies, large foreign exchange balances had accumulated during the Second World War, with the result that large and growing current account deficits were financed for several years before positive action had to be taken. In others, the favorable terms of trade during the commodity boom early in the Korean war permitted sharp increases in imports with no immediate necessity for a policy response.

However, foreign exchange reserves were eventually depleted, and/or commodity prices fell sharply. There came a point where the excess of foreign exchange expenditures over receipts required action. In most countries the political response was to adopt piecemeal, ad hoc measures. Initial reactions were also simplistic: Across-the-board restriction of import licenses to 95 percent of the preceding year's was the Turkish reaction, multiple exchange rates were a frequent response in many countries, and Chile once imposed 10,000 percent deposit requirements against applications for imports. These ad hoc policies not only were "too little, too late," but they also had political as well as economic effects that the politicians had not anticipated. When import licenses were restricted to a fraction of the preceding year's level, all those who believed that the allocation system was "unfair" to them made their case and pressured the government for an alteration of the rules. These political pressures normally proved irresistible.

To show the sorts of arguments that can be made, consider the case of imposition of import licensing based on last year's import levels. The following arguments were made by particular groups claiming a larger share: (1) Some had experienced strikes the preceding year and had therefore, they claimed, imported "unusually small" amounts; (2) some had factories that had been shut down for part of the year for mechanical reasons or while new capacity was being added and thus claimed that their preceding year's imports were "unusually small"; (3) some had only begun production during the course of the year and pointed out that the rule was unfair to new start-ups; (4) some had undertaken substantial capacity expansion in the preceding year in anticipation of larger import and output levels, and it was "unfair" to prevent them from using their new import-dependent capacity; (5) needed repairs were irregular in nature, and some firms had had none in the preceding year—last year's level of imports was therefore not representative of "true" demand; (6) potential new entrants claimed a share of import licenses, although they had not imported in the preceding year; (7) importers of pharmaceuticals and other consumer goods argued that the demand was rapidly growing and that it was "unfair" to deprive citizens of these "essentials"; (8) managers of State

Economic Enterprises claimed that government enterprises should be exempt from the regulations since they served a social purpose; (9) those wanting imports of spare parts pointed out that last year's import level was not representative of their needs; and (10) exporters argued that they should be enabled to use their foreign exchange earnings however they deemed necessary in order to earn more foreign exchange. There were undoubtedly more arguments, but the list is already long enough to make the point. It may be noted that those who had "abnormally high" imports the preceding year made no effort to surrender their import entitlements. It should also be noted, however, that some of the claimants for additional import licenses undoubtedly did have a sound economic case.

In response to arguments of unfairness by particular groups of claimants, the authorities took action. In the Turkish case imports of "luxury consumer goods" were an object of attack by almost all and were rapidly greatly restricted, if not prohibited. But even after taking measures such as these (which of course complicated the administration of the regime), the sum of claims for additional import licenses greatly exceeded the value of import reductions. The result was that imports, instead of being 95 percent of last year's level, were set at 85 percent—whereupon of course the entire process repeated itself as others made claims of unfairness and as the value of import licenses increased.

It may be noted that political response of altering the licensing system had three results: The complexity of the system greatly increased, the premium on import licenses generally rose, and opportunities for individuals and markets to profit from the increased complexity of regulations resulted. Each of these of course had economic consequences. Among them, resource misallocation increased as the import licensing system became more stringent and as the number of categories of goods increased. That in turn made the receipt of import licenses even more valuable, with the result that individuals were willing to spend more resources on obtaining them. Also exporting became less attractive still as profitable opportunities arose among import competing industries in response to increased stringency of the import regime.

Of course there were political reactions as well. Any change in the import licensing regulations led to still further cries of unfairness on the part of those who perceived that they were being discriminated against. Moreover cases came to light where private businessmen (and even occasionally managers of state enterprises) were misrepresenting their import needs. The political response was to further complicate licensing procedures and simultaneously to increase the surveillance of import licensing applications. The administrative apparatus necessary to administer import controls greatly increased. It was not uncommon to find commodities classified into capital goods, producer goods, and consumer goods, and within each of those categories commodities classified as "highly essential," "essential," "semiessential," and so on down the line. Approvals of licensing applications, which had initially been intended to take days, began taking months, and even years.

The increasingly complex licensing system gave politicians and bureaucrats a valuable political instrument that was sometimes used to reward political supporters and sometimes used for personal gain. The political usefulness of this instrument could not go unnoticed and was another factor in perpetuating it. The political reaction to evasion of state regulation, however, is to attempt to eliminate the evasion. Efforts were made to prevent the erosion of control implicit in black markets, smuggling, and over- and underinvoicing, which resulted in more detailed controls and regulations over private sector activities, with delays in license issuance, customs clearance, and other procedures, at the same time as the number of such procedures increased. Note for future reference the erosion of the authority of the state that this erosion, and to some extent corruption, entailed.

Bureaucrats and politicians were dispensing valuable rights without explicit price tags anywhere nearly equal to their market value. The consequence was that some in the political arena succumbed to the inevitable temptation to accept bribes and other rewards and favors. In at least one instance a relatively minor political party obtained the Ministry charged with issuing licenses and was able to finance itself lavishly and greatly increase its influence. In many instances contributions from industrialists benefiting from licenses became essential to financing the ruling party. In those cases reforming the system would have meant and would still mean the loss of financing for the party in power.

As these things evolved, the importance of connections with officials for successfully carrying on business increased, and efforts to curry favor with officials became a central component of private economic activity. It became jointly in the interests of bureaucrats, labor union officials, and private businessmen that the system continue. The economic community increasingly divided into the well-connected, who obtained import licenses and profited immensely thereby almost without regard to the quality of their economic activities, and those left out of the system, who operated in the "informal sector" without access to official privileges. As a consequence suspicion of officials and a belief that government represented corruption and self-seeking increased. The authority and legitimacy of the government, which had started out unchallenged in early postindependence days, was eroded.

As these processes were going on, the appreciation of the real exchange rate continued, with consequent reduced incentives for exporting. The consequent decline in exports, or at least recorded exports, had further consequences for foreign exchange reserves and for the percentage of earlier imports that could be licensed in the future. Black markets, smuggling, and other evasions of the regime mounted. Again the initial political response was to attempt to increase border surveillance, tighten customs inspections, and stamp out black market transactions. It may be noted that while some of these measures were undoubtedly partially effective, increased delays and heightened costs of obtaining inputs were also experienced by those enterprises that were attempting to carry out productive activity: Resources were increasingly diverted into obtaining the necessary permits, and otherwise reducing the costs imposed through the licensing mechanisms.

Another consequence of the increase in controls and the profitability of their evasion was that tension and suspicion between bureaucrats and private entrepreneurs increased simultaneously with the increased interdependence between them due to the businessmen's need for licenses and the politicians' need for financing. Politically one consequence was a reinforcement of the popular distrust and suspicion of markets that had underlain much early thought about development economics. Another was that bureaucrats and politicians felt compelled to develop procedures through which such suspicions could be dispelled: Licenses were no longer issued by an individual but by committees. Committee deliberations were protracted and tortured, in part because no member wanted to take the initiative to approve anything for fear that others would think he had been bribed. It goes without saying that when focus is upon proper procedure and lack of favoritism, most of the considerations pertaining to increased productivity and expanded output—the essence of economic development which was the original objective—is long forgotten. Moreover the economic payoff increasingly goes to those with the proper contacts. Those whose comparative advantage lies in being well connected or currying favor may succeed at getting import licenses or other government authorizations and hence be the most successful businessmen. Unfortunately, there is no demonstrated correlation between aptitude for dealing with the bureaucracy and that for organizing and efficiently managing productive economic activities. Doubtless some individuals who might have risen to the fore under alternative incentive schemes were unable to do so. Even among those with correlated abilities, it is likely that more of their efforts were devoted to dealing with government officials and regulations and fewer to lowering costs and improving quality and economic efficiency than would have happened in an open economy.

In most countries the "need for foreign exchange" became sufficiently obvious that it became politically acceptable, if not an imperative, to undertake policies for purposes of earning additional foreign exchange.[75] This often resulted in the provision of a more favorable exchange rate for tourists, workers' remittances, and nontraditional exports. Traditional exports continued to be eligible only for the official rate of exchange, usually with requirements that foreign exchange earnings be entirely surrendered.[76] Note that this further complicated the exchange rate regime, with further resource misallocation and additional opportunities for markets to spring up to take advantage of inconsistencies in exchange rates and other profitable activities created by the control regime.

Most governments confronted their inability to continue without some form of adjustment when export earnings had fallen sufficiently (or grown sufficiently more slowly than the demand for foreign exchange), black market exchange rates had risen far enough, and foreign exchange reserves were so low that they could no longer finance deficits. By that time the required size of the adjustment was often painfully large. Postponing adjustment, which had been politically the path of least resistance, increased both the economic and the political costs of an initially politically motivated decision not to alter the exchange rate.

By that time, however, political pressures to maintain the exchange rate had mounted. All of those receiving import licenses were opposed to devaluation because the value of their licenses would decline.[77] Businessmen, who were importing intermediate goods and raw materials for further domestic processing, declared that devaluation would only raise their costs and accomplish nothing. Producers of import-competing goods also saw no purpose to devaluation, in part because they noted that the price of imported intermediate and capital goods would increase and in part because they may have recognized that the implicit protection they were receiving would diminish. Those who were engaged in smuggling or otherwise engaged in activities to profit from the existing regime also opposed any change. Of course bureaucrats administering import licensing regulations supported the status quo.

It should also be noted that the trade and payments regime, as it evolved, created new vested interests, and hence political pressures, for the perpetuation of the system at the same time as economic pressures increased for relaxation of the system. Political resistance to change came from many quarters. One significant group consisted of those in the private sector who benefited, or believed they benefited, from receiving import licenses in exchange for payment far below the amount for which they could sell the imported goods. This even included the producers of manufactured commodities whose profits were "normal," who were in fact producing at prices and costs well above those attainable in world markets but were implicitly subsidized by cheap imports (and cheap credit). A second significant group consisted of bureaucrats who administered the import licensing system. The very complexity of the system and the perceived need for preventing "cheating" implied that it required a large technical staff to evaluate import license applications: Otherwise, imported components purportedly destined for the installation of factory machinery might in fact be resold domestically at high prices. In India bureaucrats became known as "21-day men," "3-month men," and so on. Greater prestige was attached to those whose titles indicated a longer duration. The durations referred to the time period during which the bureaucrat was permitted to delay action upon a license request without explanation. The bureaucracy that was built up under benevolent social guardian leadership itself thus came to have a large vested interest in the system. In most cases the transition to the bureaucratic-autonomous state that happened in Turkey and India went unnoticed.

A third group benefiting from the regime consisted of labor union leaders and members in industries that were built up behind a high wall of implicit and explicit protection. Wages and other conditions of employment were sometimes negotiated by unions who met little resistance when the domestic import-substituting firm had a domestic monopoly position and were sometimes mandated by government regulations. In either circumstance wages were set at levels well above those prevailing in the "informal sector," and they usually provided a great deal of job security.

Because domestic private sector industry was protected by import prohibitions and licensing, most firms had considerable monopoly power. Labor unions, whose bargaining power had been strengthened by benevolent social guardian governments, were able to negotiate with private sector firms whose incentive to resist wage increases, given their monopoly position, was relatively weak.[78] Although employment in private sector industry grew very slowly, often generating pressures for expanded public sector employment (with consequent larger fiscal deficits and other macroeconomic consequences), those fortunate enough to have employment in private sector industries became yet another group supporting economic policies. As already indicated, political parties and organizations were major beneficiaries because of the financing obtained from license seekers and also because of the power they were enabled to employ by virtue of their ability to influence the allocation of licenses.

A final group of beneficiaries of the highly restrictive trade and payments regimes accompanying import-substitution policies consisted of those who were privileged enough to be able to jump ahead of the queue in obtaining commodities in short supply due to price controls or other domestic measures taken ostensibly to curb monopoly power. In India, for example, the output of automobiles was in effect determined by the quantity of imports of various parts and components that was permitted. Prices of automobiles were controlled, and waiting lists of three years or more were common. However, civil servants and others with special claims were permitted to jump the queue and buy at the official price. Since the resale price of an Indian automobile exceeded its official purchase price for several years, there were many within government and some outside who were greatly opposed to removing price controls on automobiles.[79]

Given the large number of identifiable groups that gained from the economic controls that had been put in place, it should not be surprising that those groups became politically active to maintain their interests. In factional oligarchic states, the factions within the ruling coalition shared the spoils; in predatory states, the gains were absorbed by the ruling group or by the bureaucracy itself. In some countries the bureaucracy became a major force, and the benevolent social guardian leadership became captured by the bureaucracy.

It should also be noted that most of these interest groups had come into being *because* the exchange rate had become overvalued. Once that happened, the market reactions to the incentives provided by the regime resulted in groups of individuals who supported the continuation of the status quo. Had economic policies never made these activities possible, there would have been no pressure groups supporting them. Market responses to political decisions thus created political supporters for those decisions.

The alternative to devaluation was of course to further tighten the import regime. To a considerable degree, this was not a conscious policy decision but rather the unintended outcome of the decision not to devalue. Economic considerations forced something to be done, the political process rejected devaluation, and the result was the imposition of import licensing that was considerably more stringent than would have been undertaken on grounds of infant-industry promotion.

But these political reactions induced even more economic consequences. In general, in such circumstances there comes a point where the authorities perceive an erosion of the state (if they do not before that time make adjustments), which induces them to attempt at least some corrective measures. Earlier, piecemeal, ad hoc reform efforts are perceived to have failed, and a more systematic effort to change the system is undertaken. These episodes are so revealing that they are discussed separately in chapter 7. Suffice it here to state that, more often than not, the situation by that time is so visibly and obviously economically difficult that "politics as usual" is suspended, thus subduing, or at least diminishing, the influence of those benefiting economically from the regime.

In many countries the authorities finally accepted the necessity for some more far-reaching corrective measures than those previously undertaken. These were often accepted in return for support from the IMF, or only when there were other reasons that made the case for some change compelling. When such a stabilization program was undertaken, including devaluation, a reduction in the stringency of import licensing, and some liberalization of the regime, there was typically an interval of a year or two in which the balance-of-payments pressures (which had finally forced the change in economic policy) were lessened. Over that interval, however, the political pressures for increases in expenditures generally resulted in an upward drift in the fiscal deficit and a recurrence of the difficulties already described. This was the "stop-go" cycle, so well described by Carlos Díaz-Alejandro (1975) for Colombia, which was clearly associated with reductions in the overall rate of economic growth.

Interestingly, in authoritarian and bureaucratic predatory states that failed to alter policies in the short run, the process of long-run economic deterioration was, and in many cases still is, undermining the authority of the state. Over time the economic process therefore weakens the very instruments of power that the predatory rulers sought to use. Ultimately this perceived loss of power can motivate a change in policy, unless others dismayed by the loss of control replace the government first.

It should be noted that in all of this experience there are few recorded instances of "infant industries" that announced that they had matured and were prepared to forsake further protection. Indeed many of the processes of government were absorbed in responding to repeated pleas for increases in protection. Industries that had been awarded, usually inadvertently, sheltered domestic monopoly positions had little interest in reducing costs and few did so sufficiently (nor did they have incentive) to warrant reduced protection.

Analysis of the evolution of the trade and payments regime in developing countries illustrates several important points about the political economy of economic policy: There are economic constraints upon policymakers that can be ignored in the short run but not in the long run, policies initially adopted because of benevolent social guardian considerations may give rise to the emergence of politically influential groups in society who will support the perpetuation of those policies even if they are perceived to be ill-advised or to have outlived their usefulness, and efforts to control private economic activity in ways that run counter to behavior motivated by self-interest normally give rise to extra-legal activities and other processes that are then perceived to require additional control. When additional controls lose force, the state can deteriorate sufficiently because of economic factors to induce political reactions.

6

Political Economy of Agricultural Pricing Policies

One might think that the policy problems of the exchange rate and foreign trade regime are unusual because of the external constraint that is imposed upon national economic policy formulation. It is therefore instructive to examine a set of policies toward a domestic economic activity. Policies affecting the pricing of agricultural inputs and outputs are of considerable interest in that they shared many of the characteristics of the trade and exchange rate regime interventions, especially in their evolution. Nonetheless, they were sufficiently different in the constraints and factors guiding their evolution to provide another set of clues as to the political economy of economic policy formulation. It is highly significant that the patterns that emerge from consideration of the political economy of agricultural pricing policies are surprisingly similar to those arising from analysis of the trade regime.

In chapter 2 the agricultural disasters of Ghanaian cocoa and Sudanese cotton were alluded to. Those represent ex-

This chapter draws heavily on the findings of the World Bank's Comparative Study of the Political Economy of Agricultural Pricing Policies. The initial findings from that project were reported in Krueger, Schiff, and Valdes (1987). The synthesis of findings regarding the economic effects of agricultural pricing policies can be found in Schiff and Valdes (1992); lessons for the political economy of agricultural pricing policies are considered in Krueger (1992).

treme cases, but there is a more general proposition: Almost all developing countries have systematically discriminated against their agriculture in ways that have been detrimental to production and have depressed rural incomes relative to urban incomes. Just as the overall economic policy framework was much the same among developing countries in the initial years after independence or the Second World War, so too were agricultural policies. Even the evolution of agricultural policies has been remarkably similar, suggesting once again that there are systematic political-economic interactions at work.

Understanding of the political economy of agricultural pricing policies can best be gained by starting with consideration of their origins, followed by a brief analysis of the initial economic effects. The political responses to those effects are next examined. Finally, four political-economy questions that provide important clues for an overall understanding of political-economic interactions in the evolution of economic policy in developing countries are examined: the relative importance of direct and indirect[80] interventions and the reasons for it, the determinants of the overall degree of discrimination against agriculture, the determinants of the degree of discrimination or protection for individual agricultural commodities, and the factors that led to efforts to reform agricultural pricing policies.

Origins of Agricultural Pricing Policies

The origins of agricultural pricing policies lay partly in the same ideas of the time and partly in the same combination of motives and pragmatic responses that drove policies toward the trade and payments regime. However, an additional factor was also important: Agricultural marketing boards, inherited from colonial governments, were a ready instrument for the implementation of agricultural pricing policies in many countries.

The drive for industrialization, discussed with respect to the trade and payments regime, had as its corollary that countries' economic policies would favor industrial development at the expense of agriculture. There was also the widely held view that in a largely rural society, increased savings had to originate largely in agriculture, that private savings would not increase sufficiently, and that in a rural context, the only way to increase public savings was to tax agriculture indirectly. It was also noted that Japan had earlier implicitly taxed agriculture during her period of modernization.[81] The fact that Japanese rates of taxation had been very low relative to those in developing countries was little noted. Moreover politicians and policymakers generally believed that ignorant and irrational farmers would continue to grow their crops without regard to the prices they received for them and that depressing producer prices would not adversely affect supplies.[82] These views provided the intellectual support, or defense, of the practice of suppressing producer prices initially. Once started, however, pressures arose to increase the extent of suppression, as will be seen.

The belief that industrialization was the ultimate goal of policy was also used to argue (sometimes explicitly but more often implicitly) that the prices of food to urban residents had to be "kept low" through intervention in agricultural distribution. In part this view was grounded in appeals to income distribution considerations, since food prices were suppressed with the stated purpose of helping the urban poor.[83] In part, however, the belief that food prices should be kept low was justified on the grounds that urban wages should not rise for fear of making industrialization even more costly. As will be elaborated below, efforts to subsidize food to urban consumers were easier to finance by suppressing producer prices than they were by raising tax revenues.

While these ideologies and ideas provided the intellectual defense of discrimination against agriculture, more pragmatic political considerations also strongly influenced policy toward agriculture. As a combined consequence of ideology and political considerations, there was no single, well-defined objective regarding agriculture. In most countries political objectives were several. They included (1) the raising of revenue (to support industrialization, as already indicated, although the imperative for more revenue to support government activities general became increasingly pressing over time), (2) the support of farmers (through the distribution of input and the marketing of agricultural outputs), (3) the prevention of monopsonistic "exploitation" of farmers through the substitution of state marketing agencies, (4) the maintenance of "low prices" for (urban) consumers of food crops, (5) the "stabilization" and insulation of the domestic market from "unstable" international markets, (6) the earning of foreign exchange to "help alleviate the foreign exchange shortage" (which had arisen because of the evolution of the trade and payments regime, as described in the last chapter), and (7) the exercise of state trading powers to "offset international monopolies" and thus obtain higher prices for agricultural exports. In addition short-term political considerations led to the use of the instruments of agricultural pricing policy (especially Marketing Boards) to provide jobs for politically deserving persons and to win political support of particular groups, especially urban wage earners,[84] at critical times.

It is readily seen that these objectives were mutually inconsistent: Cheap food would imply lower government revenues; additional employment in Marketing Boards raised costs and thus either cut revenues or reduced farmers' incomes. Using domestic output to provide cheap food either reduced the supply available for export or resulted in a diversion of agricultural resources from export crops (in which there was comparative advantage) to domestic food crops.[85]

The fact that Agricultural Marketing Boards (AMBs) were already in existence in many developing countries provided the political instrument that was used for direct intervention. Agricultural Marketing Boards had initially been established as an instrument to assist expatriate planters[86] and to market commodities during the Second World War when shipping was scarce. Marketing Boards had in many instances accumulated sizable reserves in times of high international commodity prices and paid farmers more than world prices in periods of low prices. Many of them had also accumulated large cash balances.

When development policies were formulated after the Second World War, generally postindependence, these boards were already functioning agencies. Newly independent governments in effect seized these instruments but changed their purpose and functions markedly. Revenues from agencies that had been established and had their raison d'être in "assisting farmers" were altered to become instrumentalities for raising revenue for the government[87] and for buying up food crops cheaply from farmers and selling at low prices to urban workers. In part because of the belief, already mentioned, that private traders had exploited monopoly or monopsony positions vis-à-vis individual farmers, existing Marketing Boards were by law made the monopoly purchasing agent for many agricultural commodities, and the monopsonist supplier of many agricultural inputs. When Marketing Boards had not already been created, new agencies were established, ostensibly for the purpose of providing farmers with a better deal than they had received from private traders.

Market Responses to Government Policies

As with the trade and payments regimes these initial policy actions seem largely to have resulted from governments behaving, or intending to behave, as benevolent social guardians. In part because Marketing Boards were already in existence, they were simply assigned new functions: The political process seized the instruments of the state that were available and molded them to the purposes of the decision-making groups.

Even if Marketing Boards been charged only with continuing the distribution functions they already had, there would have been serious difficulties. But in most countries AMBs were given monopsony power over commodities for whose collection they had earlier been responsible alongside private traders. In addition governments either assigned AMBs the responsibility for new crops or new parastatal agencies were established to undertake their collection and distribution.

It was seen in chapter 4 that the administrative challenge was overwhelming in many countries. Nowhere were these difficulties more clearly evident than in problems that arose in the distribution of agricultural inputs and the collection of agricultural outputs. In some cases private trade was made illegal and government agencies charged with sole responsibility for collection of crops when those agencies had neither the personnel nor the facilities to undertake the task. Storage facilities were often located far from farms, with little or no capacity of either farmers or the AMBs to transport crops from farm gate to them.

Alternatively, storage facilities were themselves inadequate, and there were heavy losses of crops through rodent damage, rotting from exposure, and other problems. Delivery of fertilizers was often untimely; delivery often came well after fertilizers should have been applied, with

consequent losses in agricultural productivity and sometimes even loss of the fertilizer as natural elements resulted
in its deterioration before the next crop season. There were
even mechanical problems with paying farmers the minimum support prices that had been established by governments. Reports of delays of many months were frequent.
Thus the economic/technical demands of a well-functioning transport, storage, and collection/distribution system
often proved beyond the capabilities of government agencies in countries where private activity had been banned.

It was already noted that quality issues also presented
major problems for marketing boards and other state agricultural agencies. On one hand, if marketing boards paid
a uniform price for all grades of a particular commodity,
the tendency was for the average grade of the commodity
to fall as peasants either failed to devote the additional
resources required for higher quality or sold their high-
quality output through extralegal channels. On the other
hand, if purchasing agents were empowered to determine
the quality of the crop, the opportunity for bribery was
considerable.

Aside from the difficulties of attempting to operate a distribution system within the public sector, there were other
important economic/market reactions to initial policies. Many
of these cumulated in importance over time. Perhaps the
most important consequence was the response to the gradual decrease in the real farm-gate prices of agricultural
commodities. As the nominal exchange rate became overvalued (see chapter 5), as pressures against raising the
nominal prices of urban food intensified in the face of domestic inflation, and as the costs of marketing boards rose,
the real prices received by farmers fell. In fact farmers were
not irrational, and as the prices they received for their exportable crops fell, they shifted to production of other, more
remunerative agricultural activities or else they migrated to

the cities. As a result output of export crops grew more slowly than it otherwise would have and in some cases even fell. In Ghana the real price of cocoa by 1984 was estimated to have been about 10 percent of the price some thirty years earlier: small wonder that Ghana's exports of cocoa fell as farmers had first virtually ceased replanting, and then stopped picking the crop.[88]

As the real prices of exportables fell relative to border prices, there were other reactions. Smuggling networks arose with private agents buying up the crop and getting it across the border with higher returns. This intensified the diminution of official foreign exchange receipts and also presented officials with the challenges of attempted enforcement of policies. Where urban food prices were controlled, either the foreign exchange demands for importing food rose sharply, as in Egypt and Morocco, or exports of food commodities fell, as in Uruguay and Argentina. If the authorities were unwilling or unable to withstand the foreign exchange costs of these policies and could not or would not raise urban food prices for political reasons, their alternative was rationing. When rationing at controlled prices was the political solution, the economic response was frequently the emergence of shortages and black markets.

Political Reactions

Initially political reactions were largely a response to the evident incompetence of marketing boards in carrying out their economic functions. Farmers protested when fertilizer was delivered too late, when prices received were low and falling, and when local agents failed to collect their crops. In country after country, one reorganization or legislative amendment after another resulted as dissatisfaction with the agency's performance was great. Mention may be made of Zambia[89] and Sri Lanka[90] as particularly illuminating examples of these difficulties.

The political responses included the reorganization and often the proliferation of government agencies, with assignments of different functions to newly established agencies, followed by difficulties of coordination among agencies, followed by yet another reorganization in which agencies were consolidated. At each stage of separation and consolidation, additional employees were hired. Despite these efforts, however, the costs of marketing were rising significantly over time. By the early 1980s it was not uncommon for farm-gate prices to be less than 20 percent of the border price of agricultural commodities. More than one World Bank Structural Adjustment Loan contained, as a proviso, that prices to farmers should be at least 25 percent of the border price.

As these things happened, farmers shifted increasingly out of controlled crops into other crops. The political response was to attempt to control the distribution of additional commodities. As that happened, administrative difficulties and distribution problems intensified, and smuggling and black markets in agricultural commodities further complicated agricultural pricing policies. While the initial political responses were ad hoc and sequential, raising prices to producers in response to perceived widespread smuggling and suppressing producer prices in response to revenue needs and the desire to control inflation, an apparently inexorable process of more controls, more costly distribution, and farmers' "exit" from the state-controlled system proceeded.

At a fundamental level this inability to find a stable policy stance is relatively easily explained. Agricultural pricing policies were caught in a squeeze. On one hand, there was the demand of the government for revenue. On the other hand, revenues were falling (with random variations as international prices fluctuated) as the declining real value of export crops at domestic prices (because of exchange rate policy) and the shift out of production of agricultural outputs of commodities with suppressed prices combined with the rising costs of Agricultural Marketing Boards as payrolls expanded (both because politicians wanted the jobs for patronage reasons and because marketing boards hired more employees in an effort to correct the malfunctioning of their operations). If governmental revenue demands were met by lowering producer prices, the quantity of outputs sold to marketing boards decreased as farmers further shifted to other crops and as a higher fraction of crops was smuggled out of the country. If an effort was made to improve incentives to farmers by raising prices paid to them, revenue demands were not met.

The squeeze between the needs for revenue and output was exacerbated by downward pressure on urban prices resulting from the political desire to provide cheap food to politically vociferous urban workers. Egypt is perhaps the best-known case of subsidized food to urban consumers. In that country the expenditure involved in the government subsidy is estimated to have been in excess of 7 percent of GNP. Meanwhile the domestic price of bread was so low that it was used to feed poultry in preference to the more expensive animal feed. In Zambia, as pointed out in conversation with Robert Bates, the government was always antagonistic to rural interests. It ran down the mines and lost the support of private sector businessmen. Ultimately, its political base shrank to government workers and urban workers—most of whom *did* work for the government.

Once subsidies to urban food were established, marketing costs had risen, and farm prices were highly depressed, revenues from agriculture began to fall. The economics of agricultural pricing policy at that point confronted politics head to head. The political imperative was for low prices to urban consumers and revenue for the government; this required increased production. However, farmers shifted to alternative crops, gave up farming and migrated to the cities, returned to subsistence farming, and/ or smuggled their produce out of the country. The economic reaction had major governmental consequences. There was little government revenue, marketed supplies of food and export crops were small, and the result was losses in foreign exchange earnings and the necessity either to ration food or to use foreign exchange (already scarce from trade and exchange regime policies) to import food. A cycle often ensued around an ever-worsening trend. To be sure, some countries were able ultimately to break out of this cycle. Discussion of why and how that happened is deferred for later in this chapter and chapter 7.

Questions for Political Economy

Four aspects of agricultural pricing policies shed important light on the political-economic interactions in economic policy formulation and evolution. The first pertains to the relative importance of "direct" and "indirect" policies that affected farmers' incomes[91] relative to the prices and costs they would have faced in the absence of intervention. Direct policies include those that are adopted when the primary considerations pertain to agriculture or agricultural commodities. These include both the pricing of agricultural outputs (at farm gate and at retail) and the pricing of agricultural inputs. "Indirect" policies are those that are adopted for reasons not primarily related to agriculture but that nonetheless have a major effect on agricultural prices. The most important indirect policies are exchange rate policy and the import regime.

In the World Bank Project on the Political Economy of Agricultural Pricing Policies, a striking finding was that indirect policies often had as large, if not a larger, effect on agricultural incomes than did direct policies. Prices received by producers relative to the prices they paid for consumer goods often were a half to a third of those that would have accrued under a "neutral" policy regime, and trade and exchange rate policies alone often suppressed real returns to agricultural producers by more than 25 percent.

Nonetheless, agricultural producers' associations were often very important and very visible in lobbying and pressuring for more favorable direct interventions and silent on crucial decisions regarding indirect intervention. In Colombia, for example, the Coffee Growers' Association was regarded as one of the most powerful, if not the most powerful, interest groups in the country. Its input was clear regarding coffee pricing but entirely absent on exchange rate policy and on the trade regime.[92] This conspicuous absence of efforts to influence indirect policies raises the important political economy question as to why rational producers would have allocated their resources entirely to one set of policies at the exclusion of other, equally important, ones.

No definitive answer is possible, but many analysts in the World Bank project believed that the commitment to industrialization was so powerful politically that indirect policies could not be challenged: The ideology of industrialization provided a cover for strong discrimination against agriculture that even a powerful lobby could not affect.

Related to that is the question why governments simultaneously suppressed output prices and subsidized input prices for producers. The economist's response has typically been to assume that such policies encouraged the use of modern inputs and simultaneously offset the implicit output tax. Political scientists, however, have pointed out that it was wealthy farmers who had access to subsidized inputs; as such, politicians were able to "buy off" politically influential large farmers with subsidized inputs, while nonetheless taxing all of agriculture.[93]

The fact that export agriculture is more discriminated against than is import-competing agriculture indicates two things. First, the desire to "tax" agriculture as a measure to raise revenue for development cannot have been the only motive. If the revenue need had been the only concern, a Pareto superior policy would have been to maintain *domestic* relative agricultural prices at their international level: Real income to society would have been greater than under the import-substitution policy, and taxation would have been at the same rate for all commodities. Governments could then have subsidized domestic (urban) consumption of food by permitting domestic sales at prices below foreign sales and would nonetheless have increased their overall revenue. Second, clearly part of the basis for taxing export agriculture heavily lay in popular support for the measure. Support was based on the acceptance, by virtually everyone, that modernization was an important political goal and taxation of agriculture a necessary means to achieve it. In that sense the notion that government was a benevolent social guardian became attached to the prevailing ideas of the time. Policies then became entrenched by the support of those who were benefiting from the system.

A second question pertains to the factors that determined differences in the degree of discrimination against individual agricultural commodities. After all, if the motive for direct agricultural pricing policies was to "tax agriculture to raise resources for development," optimal policy would have been to raise revenues in a way that maximized the international value of net agricultural output subject to the revenue constraint. On the plausible assumption that resources are highly substitutable among agricultural commodities, a uniform degree of discrimination would have been optimal. That would have implied no discrimination among agricultural commodities (and perhaps discrimination against agriculture only by the exchange rate and other indirect measures).

A significant finding among the countries covered in the World Bank project was that there has been far more discrimination, or taxation, of export agriculture than against those agricultural commodities that have been competing with imported goods. Indeed import-competing agricultural commodities tend to have been protected, at least in the sense that the domestic prices of those commodities have been above those of imports at the prevailing exchange rate. Some commodities, such as rice in Colombia, have even shifted from being protected to being discriminated against, as their production increased enough so that they became exportable and were no longer import-competing goods.

A third question relates to the possible explanations, if any, for differences in the degree of discrimination against agriculture among countries. While the policies described above were universal among developing countries,[94] there were large differences in the degree of discrimination. The Ivory Coast and Kenya, for example, discriminated strongly against agriculture but not nearly as much as did Zambia and Ghana. Turkish discrimination against agriculture was much less than Egyptian.

There appear to have been two parts to the explanation. A first is the agricultural output mix between exports and import-competing commodities, already discussed. Countries whose agriculture was strongly concentrated in traditional exportable agricultural goods taxed their exports (directly *and* indirectly) far more heavily than did countries where agriculture was import competing. Thus Portugal and Korea (after 1972) had more import-competing agriculture than most other developing countries and on average did not discriminate against agriculture; by contrast, Brazil and Argentina, which were/are large net exporters, taxed agriculture heavily. In part higher taxation of export crops than of import-competing production can be accounted for by recognizing that output of exportables could decline and that export earnings could diminish for a longer period than could the output of domestic food crops. In Thailand, where the major export crop, rice, was also domestically consumed, taxation could proceed further than it could for rice in Sri Lanka and Malaysia, where the combined mandates of a low urban price and the realities of domestic supply implied that domestic production shortfalls would have to be compensated by additional imports. This led the authorities to adjust producer price rather sooner than would otherwise have been the case.[95]

Even here, one determinant of the degree of discrimination against export crops was the type of government: In factional democratic states where agricultural interests were included in the governing coalition (Sri Lanka, Malaysia, Turkey), discrimination against export crops was significantly less than in factional states where agricultural interests fell outside the ruling coalition (Egypt) or in predatory states such as Ghana. But that explanation is insufficient to account, even partially, for the difference in agricultural taxation between Turkey and Egypt or between Ghana and Ivory Coast. Here a second factor was important. As suggested by Bates (1981), when agriculturalists were in the group that attained power postindependence, the extent of taxation of agriculture diminished sharply. Factional states in which peasants or large landlords were in the ruling coalition treated the agricultural sector much better than did states in which they were not influential. Hansen (1992), in his stimulating contrast of Egyptian and Turkish development, notes that it is paradoxical that Turkey treated farmers much better than did Egypt despite the ideological commitment of the Nasser regime to help small farmers and the prevalence of larger landholdings and landlords in Turkey. His explanation: Nasser destroyed the large land-owning group, who in consequence could not represent agricultural interests.

The fourth and final political economy question is the following: If governments become entrapped in ever-more-detailed controls over agriculture, while markets increasingly escape controls, why is there not a perpetual downward spiral? The answer lies in the analysis of the political economy of reform efforts, the subject of chapter 7. Here two findings from the World Bank project, however, may be noted. They are highly significant in understanding the political economy of policy formulation and evolution.

First, and perhaps most important, was the fact that agricultural reform efforts seldom appear to have been undertaken except in the context of overall policy reform programs.[96] In the majority of cases, when discrimination against agriculture was significantly reduced, there was a reduction in direct discrimination and also in indirect discrimination, as devaluation, liberalization of the trade regime, and other policies were simultaneously undertaken. Second, as with exchange rate regimes, some reform efforts were immediately reversed, some resulted in temporary reductions in discrimination only to be followed by a reversion to earlier control patterns, and still others resulted in enduring changes in the extent of discrimination against agriculture. In analyzing the political economy of economic policy formulation and evolution, this finding provides a highly significant clue and is analyzed more fully in chapter 7.

7

Macroeconomic Political-Economic Interactions

The political-economic interactions that took place with respect to the foreign trade regime and agricultural pricing policies were also experienced in other sectors of the economy. Labor market regulations were often initiated by benevolent social guardian governments to assure workers of "fair" working conditions. The consequence, however, was the bifurcation of labor markets into "formal" and "informal" sectors. Relatively capital-intensive techniques were used in the former, with labor unions then fighting to preserve labor market regulation to the advantage of those already employed. Credit rationing, designed to provide import-substitution activities with "cheap credit," resulted in the establishment of well-functioning curb markets, where would-be borrowers (often in the informal sector) paid much higher nominal and real interest rates. Rent controls led either to markets in "key money" or to the deterioration of entire central cities.

In all of these markets the pattern was the same. Initial broadbrush regulations resulted in complaints of unfairness. The political imperative to cope with at least some of these led in turn to increasing complexity of regulations, while the economics of regulation generally led to ever-higher divergences between official prices and market prices with commensurate rewards for those who successfully evaded the controls. The growth of gray, or underground, economies eroded the authority of the state, and the increasing complexity of regulation led to larger bureaucracies and higher payoffs to those who could evade or avoid them.

It should also be noted that regulations and controls in each market spilled over into raising costs and lowering economic efficiency in other sectors of the economy. Between agriculture and the trade and exchange rate regime, for example, the fact that AMBs were high cost resulted in lower returns to farmers, which led to the further reduction in output of exportable commodities, which intensified "foreign exchange shortage" and increased the premium on import licenses. Simultaneously the fact that the real exchange rate was increasingly overvalued further lowered the return that farmers received and intensified their responses, including smuggling and evasion of the regime. Those reactions in turn prompted more efforts at controls.

The resulting reactions and inefficiencies, often combined with the economic illogic of the initial policies, led to economic performance that was deemed increasingly unsatisfactory. To a degree fluctuations in the international economy masked the trend, and economic failures generally came when world prices for export commodities were low, while the underlying unsatisfactory nature of economic performance was hidden during periods of high commodity prices.

Either way, prolonged periods of proliferating and increasingly complex controls were usually arrested at some point when it became clear that an economic correction was politically mandated. There then followed efforts to repair the system. These often consisted of reorganizations of agencies, formation of new high-level committees to "coordinate" activities, and piecemeal ad hoc measures to induce transactions into official channels.

This entire mechanism was one in which the political and economic logic of the processes that had been set in motion were at loggerheads. On one hand, the tendency for controls to proliferate and increase in complexity resulted in a greater and greater brake upon economic performance. On the other hand, the political process apparently demanded more and more, while simultaneously building in additional constituent groups supporting the economic policies that had been adopted.

The ultimate economic-political interaction occurred when economic conditions deteriorated sufficiently so that there emerged a political imperative for better economic performance. When that happened, efforts at economic policy reform were undertaken. In some cases a change in government signaled the political imperative for reform. In other instances, an economic "crisis" was deemed so urgently to require action that "politics as usual" was abandoned.

In this chapter the political-economic interactions leading up to, and conditioning, reform programs are analyzed. First, an account is given of the macroeconomic evolution of three countries with a view to suggesting the ways in which the economic and political responses described above evolve at the macroeconomic level. Thereafter three issues are addressed. First, those factors contributing to the buildup of an economic crisis are examined. Second are considered the political factors that appear to influence both the severity of the crisis that is required before action is taken and the appropriateness of corrective action. Lastly, the political ramifications of policy reform, and especially successful policy reform, are assessed.

Sequences of Macroeconomic Political-Economic Interactions

Consider first the evolution of the Indian economy. As already mentioned, there is little doubt that the leaders of the Congress party in the years preceding and immediately following independence were benevolent social guardians, who strongly believed that a Fabian socialist economic system was essential *as a means* to foster the growth of the Indian economy and to raise the living standards of the poor. Once controls were effected, however, there were several interrelated political-economic responses and interactions.

First, there were a number of unanticipated side effects of controls, as private entrepreneurs responded to the incentives with which they were confronted. Second, those private economic activities that were encouraged by the state organized to protect their interests in existing controls and to attempt to gain further measures that would benefit them. Third, a very large bureaucracy was established and grew to administer the controls, which itself became a political force.

Side effects very rapidly included a number of perfectly legal attempts to use the system for private profit, but also evasion of the control regime, outright smuggling, and the development of a "black" economy. Under the Second Indian Five-Year Plan, for example, production targets were established for a number of consumer and producer goods, based on the planners' estimates of consumer growth in demand and national savings and hence investment demand. Investment licensing mechanisms were then created, on the theory that if "too much" investment were permitted in certain lines, it would result in a "shortage" of investment in other lines of activity. In response a number of the larger private business concerns perceived that if they applied for and received investment licenses for capacity expansion in the lines of activity they were already undertaking, no new entry or competition would be possible. Since the large industrial houses were better equipped to undertake the necessary paperwork involved in applications, they initially received a disproportionate share of the new licenses. In many instances they then failed to use these licenses and were able to increase prices of their products. The initial political response to this was to attempt to restrict the access of the large houses to investment licenses, through the establishment of a Monopolies and Restrictive Practices Commission. Its assigned task was to evaluate investment license applications from the large industrial houses and to approve them only in cases where it was demonstrated that smaller firms could not undertake the investment.

The market result was "to inhibit the investment by the Large Industrial Houses either by preventing it or confining it to less lucrative areas such as heavy industry . . . and backward regions." Since these houses had earlier jointly undertaken a large fraction of all private investment, the consequence was a decline in the real rate of return on capital and for investment to be allocated to projects with a lower average real rate of return. That in turn provoked further political reactions, although it also necessitated a relaxation of the investment licensing rules.[97]

Establishment of a Monopolies and Restrictive Practices Commission was a response to one unanticipated side effect of the Indian government's economic controls. There were many others. When it was discovered that private businessmen were overstating their import requirements (because the domestic value of imports greatly exceeded their rupee foreign exchange cost if the license was granted), the number of engineers, economists, and other inspectors who had to examine the minutiae of plans for factories and equipment was greatly increased. One consequence was a lengthening of the time lag between application for investment and imports licenses and their approval.

Another was that private businessmen attempted to influence officials to grant desperately needed and profitable licenses quickly. Suspicions of corruption (and the reality) both increased greatly.[98] The consequence of the entire web of controls was the growth of a very large bureaucratic apparatus whose raison d'être was to provide permissions and to check applications from private sector individuals.

The second economic-political interaction of note was the emergence of powerful vested interests supporting those controls already in existence that benefited them and seeking additional measures. Private sector businessmen, whose profitability depended almost entirely on access to licenses, the existence of import prohibitions, and other government actions, sought in all manner of ways to insure that the political process would continue to provide these supports. Most businesses found it to their interest to establish lavishly staffed offices in Delhi and in state capitals to curry favor with officials. In addition they contributed (legally) large sums of money to support politicians. It was not long before politicians were dependent upon contributions from the private sector for their political livelihood. Again there was an irony: The benevolent guardian state that had set out to "guide" resource allocation and economic activity for the social good had become in large measure captured by those who were guided, in that politicians could not afford to offend those whom they were theoretically controlling.

The third major political-economic interaction was yet another, already mentioned, change in the political alignment of interests. As a consequence of the reactions (legal and illegal, anticipated and unanticipated) of the private sector responses to controls, the size of the economic bureaucracy grew rapidly. But the growth of the economic bureaucracy had political consequences. Hordes of bureaucrats, many living in Delhi, were dependent upon their powers to grant and withhold licenses for a livelihood. They became a political force supporting controls in their own right.

Any perceived malfunctioning of the economy became an excuse for an additional layer of bureaucracy. And every layer of bureaucracy created still further delays in the licensing process, with consequent economic inefficiencies. These inefficiencies included not only rent seeking but also the suspicion of outright corruption on the part of officials in charge of licensing. As already noted, in response to political reactions to charges of corruption (whether valid or not), committees were typically established to decide upon licensing so that individual bureaucrats would not have it within their power to "be influenced" by license applicants.

Note here the political-economic interaction. Controls generated private sector responses that led to an increase in the size of the bureaucracy and in the value of the permits being granted. The economic reaction to the creation of valuable rents was to find means—legal, extralegal, and illegal—to capture those rents. The political reaction was to attempt, through additional controls (and hence more bureaucrats), to thwart this behavior. But the value of licenses increased, so more bureaucrats were necessary and delays in approvals became even longer. Private businessmen probably did bribe in order to speed approvals to which they were entitled, but the political reaction was to increase the heavy hand of bureaucracy.

Ultimately, with growth failing to accelerate despite a tripling of the investment ratio (the Indian investment rate exceeded initial anticipations while the growth rate remained constant at the "Hindu rate of growth" of 3.8 percent annually), a benevolent social guardian state might have removed controls and tried an alternative system. But by that time the benevolent guardian state was no more. It had been replaced by the *autonomous bureaucratic* state. When in 1985 Prime Minister Rajiv Gandhi attempted to reduce the number of bureaucratic hurdles erected in the way of

most economic activities, there were 17 million bureaucrats, most of whom were more concerned about the reduction in the number of days they were entitled to
deliberate on a license application than they were in improving the functioning of the Indian economy. There were
also many private sector interests strenuously resisting any
trade liberalization or other measures that might have fostered competition. Even the labor unions were opposed to
any changes: High-paying public sector jobs might be lost
if inefficient public sector industries were forced to shed
excess labor or, more unimaginable still, close down.

It took a "crisis," six years later, to weaken the political
strength of these entrenched forces before it was politically
feasible to attempt liberalization, and even that met strong
opposition. Whether the 1991 effort at reform will be lasting will depend in part on whether the weakening of
the traditional political strength (a consequence of poor
economic performance, which in turn was the result of
controls) of those benefiting from the old system was sufficient so that the government of India can, at least for
the time being, once again behave as a benevolent social
guardian.

As a second example of sequence of political-economic
interactions, consider the Brazilian case starting in the mid-
1960s. Regardless of the form of government (military rule
from 1964 into the 1970s and then a gradual transition toward
democracy), a weak political coalition sought support by
increasing public expenditures. Because it was weak, it could
not simultaneously increase the tax base or taxation rates.
Until the late 1970s the ensuing fiscal deficits could be financed by borrowing from abroad, although domestic inflation also resulted. When in the 1980s Brazilian access to
international capital markets was cut off, domestic borrowing was substituted for international borrowing. However,
that was the same period during which there was a tran-

sition from military rule to democracy. As noted by the *Economist*,

It is hard to exaggerate the sumptuousness of the banquet the public sector gave itself to honour the coming of democracy. The politicians have not yet pushed away from the table. Federal congressmen receive both high salaries and an allowance for each day Congress sits. The 81-member Senate has 5,000 civil servants on its staff—compared with some 7,000 for the 100-member United States Senate. Things are even worse at lower government levels. The members of one municipal council get salaries equal to more than 150 times the average wage of the city's civil servants. In Paraiba, a state in Brazil's dirt-poor north-east, the state deputies voted themselves monthly salaries of over $10,000.
In all . . . between 1984 and 1987 government payroll spending—at federal, state and municipal levels—rose by 67% in real terms, or three times as fast as GNP . . .

The *Economist* proceeded to note that government savings had fallen from 12 percent of GDP in 1975 to 0 by the late 1980s, and that government investment had fallen pari passu with rising consumption and debt.[99]

Those measures in turn resulted in intensifying inflationary pressures, which ultimately resulted in a rate of inflation sufficiently high so that the implicit revenues from the inflation tax actually declined. By 1986 the unpopularity of the inflation and the "crisis of the state" (because of falling revenues) became so grave that a stabilization plan was undertaken.

Even at that point, however, the resistances to change were great. Industrial leaders opposed reform plans that would have opened the economy and threatened Brazil's highly protected import-substitution firms. Labor unions resisted any effort to reduce the degree of wage indexation. And public sector employees resisted any effort to reduce their number, finally achieving a clause in the constitution that guaranteed civil servants their jobs for life. As noted by the *Economist*, public sector expenditures continued to increase. As the various interest groups managed to maintain their powers of resistance, stabilization attempts were very short-lived, being abandoned when sufficient opposition mounted. The consequence was a cycle of temporary "reform programs" consisting of price freezes and other temporizing measures with political leaders unable to eliminate the fiscal deficit, followed by renewed acceleration of inflation.[100]

By the end of 1991 Brazil had had eleven finance ministers and six major "reform programs" announced since the cruzado plan had first been introduced in the beginning of 1986. The rate of inflation, which had reached an annual rate of 3,827 percent at its peak from the third quarter of 1989 to the third quarter of 1990 and a trough of 229 percent in 1987, still stood at 388 percent.[101]

Since there had not emerged a political coalition that could find an acceptable deficit-reduction formula, there was little prospect that the cycle would be terminated until further shifts in the political balance resulted from further economic deterioration. In the terminology of Lal and Myint, Brazil has been a weak factional state throughout the 1980s. Deteriorating economic conditions have exacerbated factionalism, rendering the body politic incapable at least thus far of responding to the deepening economic crisis.[102]

Finally, consider the case of Turkey. Discussion here is confined to the period starting in the late 1970s, although the events leading up to devaluation and stabilization plans in 1958 and 1970 were remarkably similar,[103] and the reasons for the similarity lie in the commonality of the economic-political interaction leading up to the point of crisis. In Turkey in the late 1970s, a succession of weak coalition governments was unable to establish any coherent economic policy despite mounting economic difficulties. Although there were several agreements with the IMF, fiscal deficits were increasing, inflation was accelerating, declines in imports resulted in severe shortages of such key items as heating oil and gasoline, and massive labor unrest resulted in widespread strikes. By late 1979 the rate of inflation had reached 100 percent in a country where there was little indexation and where key groups, including the civil service and the military, were achieving nominal income adjustments only after long lags. Real output had fallen for two consecutive years, and hardships resulted not only from these phenomena but even from the lack of heat in the severe Anatolian winter.

In this context the power of the various groups in the coalitions was severely weakened. The economic decline had reduced their effectiveness, and the economic crisis in effect suspended "politics as usual." In that environment Prime Minister Demirel, who headed the weak coalition government, asked Turgut Özal to take charge of economic policy. Working with only a very small—estimated at ten—number of technocrats, Özal put together a far-reaching economic reform program. That program consisted not only of short-run stabilization measures (which were effective in bringing the rate of inflation down to about 35 percent two years later) but also of sweeping economic reforms.

Over the next five years the real exchange rate depreciated greatly, virtually all quantitative restrictions on imports were removed, the autonomy of public sector enterprises was markedly reduced and budget constraints were imposed on them, financial markets were liberalized, and so on. Although the military took over from the civilian government in September 1980, they retained Özal in charge of economic policy. When elections were held in 1983, Özal was elected Prime Minister, despite opposition from the military.

On most fronts the Turkish economic reforms were successful.[104] Real economic growth gradually accelerated, reaching an average rate of over 6 percent in the last half of the 1980s. For present purposes what is interesting is that economic decline resulted in an erosion of the usual political base that many groups resisting change normally had. The result was that a group of technocrats was empowered to carry out reforms. As those reforms succeeded, political support developed for the government, which was then enabled to carry its program further.

Thus inappropriate economic policies from earlier years had resulted in a coalition of economic interests in support of those policies in a factional democratic state in Turkey in the late 1970s. However, economic policies were so unpopular that the support for the politicians dwindled, as more and more groups came to believe that continuation of the status quo ante would harm them. A benevolent social guardian government could then attempt to reform economic policies. The success of those reforms in turn brought support for the government, thus permitting almost a decade of autonomy in economic policy making.[105] All observers noted that the politics of economic policies regarding the roles of the private and public sectors had been inalterably changed during the 1980s. It had earlier been almost sacrosanct in Turkey to regard State Economic Enterprises and the government as the instrument for social good and to suspect private enterprise as contributing little or nothing to social welfare. The experience of the 1980s persuaded most Turks that private enterprises could indeed produce and export. This in turn resulted in a permanent change in economic policies pertaining to the role of the state in economic activity.

The list of country experiences in which political and economic variables interacted in ways that changed both the nature of economic policy and the type of government could be considerably lengthened. Failed Korean economic policies of the 1950s gave way to Presidents Park Chung Hee and Chun Doo Hwan and an era during which there was a benevolent social guardian type of government in Korea. The very economic success of that government, however, created a large middle class, fully aware of its political impotence. The consequence was a political upheaval in which the authoritarian benevolent social guardian was replaced by a democratic factional state. The consequences of that change for Korean economic policies and prospects have not yet become clear. The Taiwanese story is very similar. Latin American cycles of populism–conservative autocratic government have already been mentioned. Even Eastern European governmental change was closely related to the failed economic policies of the earlier regime.

Buildup to Economic Crisis

Most of the ingredients of crisis have already been discussed. What remains to be done is to note their macroeconomic interactions and implications. Regardless of the form of government—benevolent guardian, predatory authoritarian or bureaucratic, or factional—the political process typically demanded more resources than were available from tax revenues in the early stages of growth. Whether these resources were intended to increase productive public investment, as in benevolent guardian states, or to satisfy the particular interest groups in the factional coalition in power was irrelevant. The fact was that pressures were such that almost all countries incurred fiscal deficits of a magnitude larger than was sustainable without some degree of inflation in excess of the world rate.

The tendency for growth to decelerate, resulting from the consequences of the economic policies adopted, and also the increasing incentives for evasion of control regimes tended to slow down the rate at which government resources grew. Simultaneously the growth rate of demands upon those resources remained constant, or even increased.

In some instances, foreign assistance filled part of the gap between perceived demands and the availability of domestic resources for governmental purposes. In Korea in the 1950s, for example, the negotiating process that determined the level of U.S. assistance was essentially a "gap-fill" one.[106] Even so, foreign assistance was usually at levels that permitted larger government expenditures than would otherwise have been possible but still left sufficiently large excess of expenditures over aid-inclusive revenue that inflation resulted. More generally, more foreign assistance permitted greater short-term responses to political demands for increased government expenditures and did little to close the resource gap or to address the long-term imbalance between the political demands of key constituencies and the supply of resources to the state. In other instances, as during the Korean war, high commodity prices yielded abnormally large governmental revenues, which were immediately spent upon public investment or consumption goods.[107] Even in countries that initially were relatively fiscally conservative, such as India, there were pressures to accelerate public spending, although they initially were much better contained than in countries where inflation was more acceptable.[108]

There are elements in both the political and the economic process itself that intensify the excess demand for public expenditures over time. On the political side there are obvious ones: Inevitably interest groups demand better treatment over time. Workers want real wage increases, agricultural producers want higher real prices for their outputs, while urban dwellers resist any increases—nominal or real—in food prices, public sector employees want growing real incomes, and all groups want increased social insurance and improved benefits from other public programs.

Moreover, once inflation was ongoing, there were asymmetric pressures: On one hand, resistance to increases in nominal prices of subsidized consumer goods (food, electricity, transport services) was strong, so the real prices charged by governments tended to fall over time. On the other hand, civil-servants' wage demands were normally couched in terms of indexation plus and real government expenditures consequently tended to increase on that account as well as because of growing numbers of public sector employees. The gap between revenues and expenditures thus tended to grow over time simply as a consequence of inflation, quite aside from other reasons.

On the economic side the built-in tendencies for growth to decelerate once controls were operative (and the increased demand for public sector employees to administer increasingly complex control system) have already been described. In many countries the political imperative to achieve economic growth therefore required ever-increasing rates of expenditure in order to maintain constant rates of growth in the face of falling real returns to incremental resources.

Consequently there emerged a squeeze on resources in the public sector. There were three ways in which this could be resolved: borrowing or otherwise obtaining resources from abroad beyond those already budgeted (e.g., foreign aid), domestic deficit financing, and fundamentally altering economic policies.

Typically the political process first attempts to resolve the imbalance between expenditures and revenues through resort to foreign resources.[109] In some instances, when that avenue finally closes down, policy changes are undertaken. In other instances, domestic financing of the public sector deficit is substituted for foreign resources once the latter are no longer available.

Resort to foreign resources may in itself be of several varieties. First, there are, or were, the pressures that could be placed by a country deemed politically important on a major donor to provide additional resources. This was certainly the strategy of President Sygman Rhee in Korea in the 1950s. Often these resources were sought on the ground that the client state would otherwise be politically destabilized.

Second, for middle-income countries there was resort to foreign borrowing from private sources. This was a major avenue for obtaining excess resources in many developing countries in the 1970s and early 1980s. Mexico, for example, experienced a major increase in export earnings from both the discovery of oil fields and the increased price of oil in the 1970s. Even during that period governmental resources were augmented by borrowing from foreign private commercial banks. When the growth in government resources stopped in the early 1980s, borrowing from private sources accelerated.[110]

At some point of course foreign lenders are unwilling to continue extending credit, at least at past rates. They observe mounting indebtedness with little growth in foreign exchange earnings and more rapid growth in the demand for imports. In these circumstances major questions arise about a country's creditworthiness and, at a minimum, the terms upon which borrowing can take place are hardened and the amounts extended are reduced. For a time resort may be had to increasing short-term indebtedness through suppliers' credits and other instruments. Even those high-cost sources of funds disappear, however, when arrears begin mounting.

In Turkey, for example, mounting short-term indebtedness was usually the symptom of underlying difficulty. The government would issue obligations to foreigners (including foreign-exchange denominated domestic deposits) at increasingly costly terms. Thereafter suppliers' credits would mount, as would delays in licensing imports. Finally, even suppliers' credits were unavailable. Prior to the foreign exchange crisis at the beginning of 1980, it was reported that foreign exchange had become so scarce that Turkish civil servants in embassies overseas had in some instances not been paid for several months.

Throughout this process imported goods of course become increasingly scarce in the domestic economy. In the Turkish case, where there is no domestic source of crude oil, the increasingly impaired capacity of the transport system resulted in major economic dislocations, thus precipitating the crisis. In other countries, however, the higher economic costs of increasing autarky are accepted, and when foreign resources are no longer available, the excess of government expenditures is financed by domestic borrowing with accelerated inflation as a consequence. This seems to have been the pattern in Brazil, Argentina, Mexico (at least until 1982), and a large number of African countries. In yet other countries, including Myanmar and India, slow economic growth seems to have been accepted as an inevitable fact of life.

Even when contracting imports are the perceived source of crisis, there are two alternatives. One alternative is to undertake a genuine reform effort, as will be discussed further below. The other is to seek foreign resources from the multilateral lending institutions in return for short-term corrective measures.

This latter route, part of the "stop-go" cycle, has been resorted to in many circumstances. The authorities have either perceived their difficulties to be short term, a consequence of sharp drops in the prices of their primary commodity exports (or bad weather and a consequent reduction in supplies of major export crops), or alternatively have been sufficiently desperate to agree to a stabilization program in order to obtain additional resources from the multilateral lending institutions quickly. In neither of these cases have reforms addressed fundamental issues. Hansen (1975), for example, describes how the Egyptian authorities in 1963 agreed to an IMF stabilization program, including devaluation, while simultaneously taking offsetting measures so that few domestic prices were significantly affected. In other countries, such as Turkey in 1958 and 1970 and India in 1966, measures were taken to try to mitigate the undesired consequences of earlier policies, but those policies were not viewed as having been fundamental in contributing to the emerging crisis. Hence, as soon as resources were once again available, "controls as usual" resumed.

What Determines Whether to Reform?

Most reforms seem to take place in one of two circumstances: Either a new government comes to power or a perceived economic crisis prompts action. To be sure, these two events are not mutually inconsistent: A new government is more likely to result when performance is perceived to be unsatisfactory, and that perception is more probable when an economic crisis takes place.

A first problem then is to determine what is, and what is not, a crisis. No satisfactory answer has yet been given: Rates of inflation that in one country provoke immediate policy responses are not even criticized in other countries, and the absence of critical goods such as medicines and petroleum has been withstood for years in some countries, while inducing an immediate response in others. Conditions in Ghana and in Sudan probably merit the adjective "crisis" for any date from 1979 onward. Ghana's reform effort effectively began in 1983; Sudan, like Brazil and Argentina, inaugurated several sets of policy changes, none of which were adequate to correct the underlying economic difficulties.

Moreover, one cannot define crisis based simply on observations of when governments do act to change policies: One may think of the objective economic situation as representing the demand for policy change (the demand being smaller when underlying economic conditions are more satisfactory); the supply of policy reform is a function, at least partially, of the government's ability to carry it out. When a governing coalition is fairly cohesive and commands a reasonable majority, policy reform may come at an early stage in the process of economic deterioration. It may be argued, for example, that the rapid Korean reaction to the economic problems induced by the oil price increase of 1973–74 was as much a response to "crisis" as were the much later reforms of other countries. The fact that the government was cohesive and had the political resources permitted it to act rapidly.

By contrast, in many countries the economic difficulties are in part reflective of a political impasse, where the government is sufficiently weak so that decision making is incapacitated. In these circumstances the initiation of a reform program must await the juncture at which the economic difficulties have become so severe that "politics as usual" is no longer possible. In Turkey, for example, the economic crisis of the late 1970s was little worse at the end of 1979 than it had been at the end of 1977, except in the sense that it had persisted for two years longer. The difference was that by the end of 1979 the extremity of the economic crisis had weakened the political influence of the groups that had earlier contributed to a political impasse.

This process of weakening normal political resistances can come about in several ways. On one hand, there are countries in which the severity of the economic difficulties per se results in a gradual consensus that "something must be done." On the other hand, there are countries in which the precipitating factor is what has been termed "the withering away of the state": [111] The point at which the erosion of the state's authority and capacity to act has proceeded so far that the purpose of policy reform is, in effect, to begin to restore the authority of the state.

With these considerations in mind, we are now ready to link the discussion of policy reform to the various governmental types discussed in chapter 4. At one extreme, a reasonably "strong" government with popular support (e.g., a benevolent social guardian such as Korea) confronts a change in economic circumstances that in the long run requires action. It has the political resources to undertake action *and the technocratic support to take appropriate actions.* At the other extreme is a highly divided factional state in which there is a spiralling economic deterioration, perhaps punctuated occasionally by short-term improvements when world prices of major exports rise sharply and by sudden apparent worsening of the situation when commodity prices drop. In such a factional state it is, or is believed by the leadership to be, infeasible to reach sufficient agreement to undertake a determined course of action, and the crisis drags on, with the factional state continuing. A change of government may bring about an announced set of changes, but any reasonable economic analysis would reach the verdict of "too little, too late."

In between there are a number of scenarios. The bureaucratic-authoritarian state's authority breaks down as economic conditions deteriorate; this provides an opportunity for the present leader (or a new one) to designate a new finance minister, who then has an opportunity to put together a reform program. Depending on the sort of program chosen, the outcome may be short-term relief, with reversion to the stop-go cycle, or it may be longer-term reforms.

One could also turn the analysis around. An initially successful reform program may provide a "honeymoon period" during which those strong political interests opposed to reform are to a considerable extent neutralized. If additional policy measures (and good luck) then provide additional economic gains, support for the reforms may strengthen and opponents are weakened. New interests emerge favoring the altered economic policies.

Such a program may have been carried out by an authoritarian benevolent social guardian. But if the program is successful over the longer term, rising incomes and an emerging and strengthened middle class may demand greater participation in the political process. At that stage economic success may bring about the transformation of the state to a factional democratic form.

It is relatively straightforward to point to instances of each of these economic-political interaction sequences. The Korean reforms of the early 1960s were undertaken by a new government, whose support came to be based largely on the success of its economic policies. It was able to make necessary policy adjustments because of that support, and economic growth was rapid with the emergence of a greatly strengthened middle class. Ultimately many more groups in society voiced their desire for political participation, so that economic success laid the groundwork for political transformation to a democratic factional state. The Chilean experience in moving from Salvadore Allende to Augusto Pinochet (after failed economic policies) to democracy (after successful policies) represents a similar pattern.

Turkish reforms in 1980 could be undertaken only after the usual political pressure groups had lost their influence as a consequence of the extreme economic difficulties the country was experiencing. When the reforms were undertaken, there was a "honeymoon period" in which the government was released from the usual political constraints. In fact the military takeover further strengthened the hands of the technocratic economic reformers, and gave time for further actions and for the effects of reforms to be felt. By the time of elections in 1983, support for the reforms was sufficient to permit their architect to regain power. Until the latter 1980s the party in power derived increased strength from the success of reforms, although other issues undermined its support.

Brazil's experience represents yet another pattern. There the factional state has rendered all coalitions incapable of undertaking sufficiently far-reaching economic policy changes to permit a fundamental reversal of that country's economic difficulties. The consequence is that the political leadership, under continuing pressure because of poor overall economic performance of the economy, has frequently appointed new economics teams, each of which has had insufficient authority to bring about a policy reform program that could have reversed the country's downward spiral.[112]

Many African countries appear to have reached a similar impasse. As Bates and Collier (1993) document the Zambian experience, economic failures resulted in the disaffection of an ever-increasing number of groups in society. Since the ruling party had an ever-narrower base of support and hence a more precarious political existence, its ability to undertake major policy changes was continually weakened.

In developing countries where elections are the norm, changes of governments have been accompanied by a mandate to change economic policies. Such was the case in Sri Lanka in 1977, when electoral disgust with heavy-handed bureaucratic microeconomic interventions led to a new government that undertook a fairly far-reaching liberalization of the economy.[113] Peru's changes of governments have also frequently been accompanied by mandates from the voters for changes in economic policy.

What Determines the Nature of Reforms?

The precise package of reforms undertaken clearly depends on a variety of factors. First, any government is dependent on some reasonably well-defined groups for support, and reforms will normally not greatly weaken those groups. Thus Argentine reforms could be undertaken but did little to offset past discrimination against agriculture because agriculture was not part of the governing coalition. By contrast, Sri Lankan governments were dependent in part on the support of small farmers; Sri Lankan policies therefore were much more sympathetic to the interests of that group, although not to the interests of rubber and tea plantations (where expatriate managers ran large-scale operations).

Some changes of government have been reasonably clearly identified with changes in predominant groups in the governing coalition. In Pakistan, for example, the Bhutto government represented a very different group of economic interests than did the military governments that preceded and succeeded it. Economic policies were generally populist under Ali Bhutto and more orthodox under military governments. Hence, when Bhutto came to power, his government reversed earlier policies, and when General Mohammed Zia ul-Hag succeeded Bhutto, he once again reversed policies.[114] Thus agricultural marketing was nationalized under Bhutto, and denationalized under Zia as power changed hands.

In cases such as these it is a shifting political consensus that drives the nature of the reform package. It is important to recognize that the shift in political consensus may be, and usually is, itself a consequence in part of voter reactions to the economic consequences of existing economic policies. But there is an important point to be noted here, especially in the context of an essay considering the endogeneity of political economic interaction. There is potentially a large role for technocratic inputs in policy reform. In countries in which policy reforms have been undertaken, technocrats have typically had a fairly large input. In some instances technocrats have been unable to influence certain key variables because of political constraints confronting the political leadership, yet they have had extraordinary power over other policies.

In part, this power has emanated simply from the desperation of the politicians at the point when reform has been sought. In part it has come about because the "window of opportunity," previously discussed, removes many of the normal political constraints and permits a freedom of action for technocrats that is not possible when it is "politics as usual." A third factor, however, also contributes. That is, because of the need for external assistance at the time when policy reform is undertaken, and the evident need for improved economic performance, those whom the political leaders believe to have appropriate economic understanding have unusual powers.

To a degree, there is an element of chance in the formulation of reform programs. The ruling political leadership may choose technocrats better or worse equipped for carrying out their mission. It has already been suggested that a more realistic alternative to the Cruzado Plan might have had a better chance of success. Likewise, in the late 1970s, the opening of the capital account before tariffs were removed was clearly a "technocratic mistake" in Argentina and in Chile.[115] As economic understanding of policy reform grows, the ability of economists to contribute their understanding to the formulation of reform programs with improved long-term prospects of success will improve.

In many countries it is a small group of technocrats who in effect determine the main outlines of policy reform. In Turkey it is estimated that fewer than ten persons (all technocrats under the leadership of Turgut Özal) knew the content of reforms before they were announced.[116] In Korea the deputy prime minister (who was head of the economic planning board) was head of the economics team and had enormous economic power. In Chile, Indonesia, Taiwan, Argentina under the military in the late 1970s and again under democratic governments in the late 1980s, Brazil for the Cruzado Plan, Mexico in the latter half of the 1980s, India in 1991, and Ghana after 1984, technocrats were similarly important. In most of these instances the power and authority of the technocrats persisted well after the initial reforms and in many cases lasted for many years.

In an important sense technocrats so empowered become, or can become, benevolent social guardians during the reform process. Ironically, if their initial reform package is reasonably sound and if external circumstances are not extremely unfavorable, they may be enabled to transform a bureaucratic authoritarian state back into a benevolent social guardian state. Moreover, as already suggested, successful reforms may in the longer term result in political pressures for the introduction of a more pluralistic regime.

These windows of opportunity are even more crucial when it is recognized that for most periods of time, political-economic interactions take place in ways that can be little influenced by economists and the dismal science. While better or worse economic support may underpin the particular ways in which populist or orthodox programs are carried out (and technocratic mistakes, especially in the latter, can make a big difference), political leaders' predispositions, needs to "reward" certain groups, and imperatives to mollify other groups normally determine the overall architecture of economic policy. Those leaders are very likely to select finance and economics ministers who are in accord with those predispositions. Those individuals in turn will normally seek advice from those around them who are sympathetic with their overall approach. Orthodox economists would, for example, have had little chance to be heard under the Peruvian government of Alain Garcia, while populist economists would not have been heard under that of Pinochet.

Windows of opportunity in which the normal political processes are enfeebled or paralyzed therefore become crucial in determining economic evolution. The Argentine reforms of the late 1970s stand as a reminder of what can happen when technocrats themselves fail to diagnose the problems at hand sufficiently. In that instance failure to recognize the extent of water in the tariff, and the degree to which inflationary pressures could not be contained without more corrective action regarding the fiscal deficit, doomed the efforts of a very committed and dedicated group of technocrats who had full support of the military government. When the prefixed exchange rate finally had to be abandoned, it was clear that the reform program had been doomed from the start.

What Determines the Success of Reforms?

One of the more discouraging features of reform programs has been the limited number of success stories. As noted earlier, more countries have experienced a reversion to their earlier economic difficulties within two or three years after the beginning of a reform program than have successfully entered a period of long-term improvement in economic performance.[117]

It has already been noted that technocratic mistakes may jeopardize the prospects for improved economic performance following the launching of a policy reform program. Likewise bad luck in the form of poor weather or drastic drops in export prices may doom a reform program that might, under other circumstances, have worked. However, it is not the purpose here to provide an economic analysis of the determinants of the success of reform.[118] What political economy can contribute to understanding is the recognition that the governing coalition's perceptions of the need for reform and its ability to take the necessary measures can critically influence the package of policy measures that are undertaken. When, as in Egypt in 1963 or India in 1966, the government is strongly entrenched and the leadership does not perceive any threat to long-run economic performance, announcements of policy reforms must be treated with considerable skepticism: Programs are very likely to be minimal, attempting to gain resources from the multilateral lending institutions and foreign creditors rather than to lay a basis for improved economic performance.[119]

Likewise, when the government is best characterized as a "factional state," in the Myint-Lal terminology, with weak support and an imperative to maintain the support of all its constituent groups, it is unlikely to be *able* to develop a reform program that offers sufficient prospect of change in underlying economic policy: One or more groups will perceive the threat to themselves to be too great, defect from the governing coalition, and bring the government down.

In the former case what is needed before successful reform can be attempted is persuasion that existing economic policies are not compatible with prospects for long-term growth. In the latter case, regardless of how many groups in society believe that underlying economic policies do not offer promise of improved performance, policy reform cannot be undertaken until existing political forces are realigned. As already mentioned, that can happen through an election (or a coup d'etat) bringing a new (reformist?)

government to power, or through the "withering away of the state," which erodes the ability of the individual interest groups to undermine the government.

When either the commitment to the reform process or the ability of the government to carry out reform is highly dubious, businessmen and citizens will perceive it. In those circumstances, for reasons already discussed, the prospects for maintenance of altered policies will dim simply because the response to them will be dulled by virtue of that skepticism. But the very fact that the response to altered signals is diminished means that there will be a longer period of transition, and thus more economic discomfort, than would occur if decision-makers were persuaded that policy changes would be lasting. When that happens, there is more time and opportunity for opposition to reforms to attack it, thus weakening support for the government and increasing doubts as to the viability of the program.

Ironically then it can be the perception of a weak governmental will or ability to carry out reform that can motivate economic behavior, delaying decisions based upon altered policies until evidence mounts that those policies will persist. But the decision to delay any response, based upon perceptions of the political process, results in a prolongation of the period of transition with attendant stagflation. That in turn provides political ammunition for the opponents of reform, which further strengthens the perception of unsustainability of the reform program.

By contrast, a government perceived to be committed to reform and with sufficient power (through an authoritarian regime, a benevolent social guardian with support, or a democratic election) to maintain the new policy regime has an advantage in undertaking reform: The responses will be more rapid simply because the reforms are more credible.

8   Conclusions

In the preceding chapters I have attempted to show that the economic ramifications of political variables, and the political ramifications of economic variables, are sufficiently great so that many aspects of economic policy cannot be satisfactorily analyzed without taking both political and economic elements into account. Enough has been learned so that it is relatively straightforward to point to mechanisms of political-economic interaction that are important and cannot be ignored in either political or economic analysis. But there also remain a great many questions whose answer will require a great deal of further research.

I wish briefly to speculate on two important questions to which answers must, at best, be highly tentative. A first concerns the cycles of policymaking. The second considers the evolution, over time, of types of states, based on their interaction with economic policy.

Cycles of Policy-making

Political scientists have analyzed the Latin American political cycle of populism, military (or otherwise oligarchic) government populism. Economists have analyzed the stop-go cycle of expansion-cum-increasing current account deficits, recession-cum-devaluation-and-stabilization and import compression, followed by renewed economic (and import) expansion. Each group has tended to treat these phenomena as belonging entirely to its domain of analysis. The central insight of political economy, as it relates to economic policy and economic policy reform in developing countries, is that much of both the political and the economic cycles is endogenous. The economic consequences, intended and otherwise, of political decisions alter the political balance. The political consequences of economic policies are equally important.

Some years ago Jagdish Bhagwati and I suggested that it might be useful to study the evolution of foreign trade regimes across countries by characterizing those regimes as being in one of five phases.[120] Phase 1 was described as that period during which (trade and exchange) controls were fairly uniform and across the board. Phase 2 was then a period during which controls were increasing in complexity as there were ad hoc reactions to various undesired economic responses. Phase 3 was a period of reform: It might be a "tidying-up" of the regime, or it might consist of more far-reaching policy changes. Either way it was described as a period during which the proliferation of controls had reached a point where the system had become unmanageable and hence there was a decision to change. Phase 4 was described as a period during which continued liberalization and relaxation of controls persisted, while phase 5 was described as the situation when there were few trade and exchange rate controls.

Bhagwati and I argued that countries, once in phase 1, gravitated naturally to phase 2 for a variety of reasons, and that phase 3 thereafter more or less inevitably followed. We then noted that the sequel to phase 3 might be either a "reversion," as we called it, to phase 2 or a move to phase 4. Phase 4, we thought, could end either in phase 5 or in a reversion to phases 1 or 2. This stylization of phases proved highly useful in characterizing the evolution of trade and payments regimes. Later on, somewhat to my surprise, analysts of agricultural pricing policies in developing countries found it equally useful to trace the history of agricultural pricing in a number of countries.[121]

The political-economic interactions discussed in these lectures, however, provide a reason why the phases may have been a descriptively accurate way of tracing the dynamics of that evolution. The initial imposition of controls (phase 1) sets into motion economic responses that to a considerable extent defy the intent of those imposing the controls. Politicians' responses, as they attempt to control the economy and to thwart the market, result in phase 2. Unsatisfactory economic performance then sooner or later generates a political mandate to "try something" to change the outcome and that motivates a move to phase 3.

If the underlying political-economic situation is sufficient so that the reform program is sufficiently far-reaching and credible, underlying economic performance can improve (phase 4). That can permit further liberalization, while simultaneously strengthening the political influence of new groups (e.g., exporters) and generating popular support because of improved overall economic performance. If, once that process has begun, an external shock (the oil price increase of 1973) or other circumstances result in economic difficulties, politicians may decide to reinstate control mechanism (reversion to phase 2). This clearly happened in Brazil in 1973–74, for example. If, instead, politicians are committed to reforms, liberalization may proceed, as happened in Korea.

Whatever the outcome, it seems clear that there is an economic-political logic to the evolution of controls once they are initially imposed. The period of proliferation may be longer or shorter, depending on circumstance and political strengths of different groups. The reform program may come sooner or later and be stronger or weaker, but the interactions between markets and efforts to evade controls and politicians and efforts for the state to maintain control seem to imply that there is an underlying process that leads from phase 1 through phase 2 and then, at some point, to phase 3.

Whether phase 3 is followed by further liberalization and phase 4 is determined by a number of factors, including the ability of the technocrats to put together an economically sensible program, the credibility of the government that the program will be maintained, and the occurrence of favorable or unfavorable external (and internal) shocks during the transition period. When transition to phase 4 takes place and proceeds, it can result in a realignment of political factors, providing political support and therefore increased belief in the sustainability of the new set of economic policies. If that "positive dynamic" between markets and politics can be achieved, improved economic and political performance may continue for an extended period of time.

Is There a Political-Economic Evolution?

Politicians' decisions as to economic policy are an outcome of the existing balance of political forces, which are themselves a function in part of the state of the economy. Those decisions, however, have economic consequences that affect not only resource allocation and growth but also the balance of political influence. This is true of both microeconomic (or sectoral) policies and of macroeconomic policies.

Economic success can create a political basis for support of a government, while economic failure can erode not only that basis but threaten the powers of the state itself. With economic failure the change in political equilibrium can bring about an intensification of controls and intervention, with still further downward (or, at first, simply growth-retarding) pressure on economic activity and more political consequences. Alternatively, or at some point in this downward spiral, the normal political influences become reduced in importance relative to the political imperative to halt, if not reverse, the downward cycle.

One of the questions that has been raised by both political scientists and economists has been the relationship between economic policies (and the ability to change them), on one hand, and the type of government, on the other. Myrdal (1968) first raised this in the context of "soft" states and "hard" states. In his analysis only "hard" states (e.g., Korea and Taiwan, which he identified as dictatorial) could undertake the necessary economic policies to achieve very rapid economic growth. More recently the question has arisen as to whether satisfactory policy reform can be undertaken in democratic societies.[122] Observers have noted that the Chilean government, during the reform period, was dictatorial, and have also cited Taiwan and Korea as reformers.[123]

Although the analysis of economic-political interaction is not yet sufficiently well-developed to provide an answer to that question, events of the 1980s have suggested some possible dynamics. Recall that the "typical" developing country witnessed its initial economic policies being put in place by a "benevolent social guardian" state, whether that state was democratic or authoritarian under a charismatic nationalist leader. The economic policies of control led rapidly to the proliferation of controls, which in turn resulted in an increased size and influence of the bureaucracy.

In many countries the "governing coalition" then became the politicians, bureaucrats, businessmen, labor union leaders, and intellectuals who supported and benefited from these interventionist, control-oriented policies. The benevolent social guardian state in many cases was transformed into a bureaucratic-authoritarian state, even in countries such as India where the democratic ethos was strong. But economic policies were such that the political mandate for a rising real standard of living was insufficiently met, which in time began eroding the coalition and the bureaucracy.

In some instances (Sri Lanka) an election resulted in a reversal of policies. In some countries palliative reforms were undertaken, and a stop-go cycle lasted for a period of time. In some cases members of the governing coalition became convinced that the past economic policies had failed and that radical changes were necessary (e.g., Korea and Taiwan early on and Mexico and Turkey more recently). When that happened, living standards started to rise, and political-economic interaction took on some new dimensions.

In the places where those policies have proceeded the most, there are two features of note. First, under the economic policies that have generated rapid growth, the political response to economic success has tended to strengthen support for economic policies. But second, and equally important, as economic success has continued and living standards have risen, there have been increasing demands for participation in government. Pressures for democratization of political institutions have finally become irresistible. In Korea, Taiwan, and Chile this process has played out in ways in which economic success has finally resulted in an impetus for political change.

To end on a highly speculative and probably overoptimistic note, it may be hoped that as economists learn how to avoid the bad mistakes in policy reform, the number of economically successful reform programs will increase. As those programs succeed and change internal politics, momentum for further liberalization and rapid economic growth will perhaps accelerate. With it, rising living standards could provoke calls for greater democracy. Should the combination of economic policies that generates high living standards and democratic political institutions prove to be a stable one, it would represent the end point of a long, and in some countries convoluted, process of political-economic interaction.

Notes

1. See Cardenas (1990), pp. 16ff, for a description of the economic situation at that time.

2. Kaufman (1988), p. 79.

3. Stryker (1990), p. 138.

4. Data are from International Monetary Fund, *International Financial Statistics*, 1991 Yearbook, p. 115. The average of the annual rates of increase of wholesale prices was used to calculate the decadal rate.

5. It should be noted that a country can have had an interval of acute inflation during chronic inflation, and of runaway inflation during a period of acute inflation. Brazil, for example, is deemed to have had acute inflation over the entire 1975–89 period, with runaway inflation in 1976, 1983–85, and 1988–89. Had the IMF had data through 1991, the period of acute inflation would have been extended.

6. See MacKenzie (1989) for a discussion of alternative indicators of the public sector deficit.

7. International Monetary Fund, *International Financial Statistics Yearbook*, 1991, pp. 154–55.

8. Data from International Monetary Fund (1987).

9. Edwards (1989), p. 101.

10. Bhagwati and Srinivasan (1975), p. 129.

11. See, for example, Krueger (1975).

12. World Bank, *World Development Report*, 1987, p. 89.

13. While history suggests that some moderate rate of taxation on agriculture may facilitate the development process, the major contribution of agriculture to growth is through increasing productivity in such a way that agricultural supplies to urban areas are increasing at a rate sufficient to support the growing urban population without increases in food prices.

14. Bardhan (1984). Data are taken from tables 13 and 14, pp. 102–104.

15. See, for example, the fascinating account of Nimal Fernando, "The Political Economy of Mahaweli," mimeo for the World Bank, 1987. Fernando documents change after change in Sri Lankan regulations in response to the inability of authorities to deliver inputs and purchase outputs in a timely fashion. Transport sites, transport capacity, storage capabilities, difficulties with payments mechanisms, and a variety of other problems plagued those attempting to carry out mandated public operation of agricultural distribution.

16. See Krueger and Aktan (1992).

17. See Krueger (1988) for further analysis.

18. See De Soto (1989) for a vivid description and analysis of this phenomenon in Peru.

19. See, for example, the numbers reported in Krueger (1983).

20. See Bardhan, ch. 8, for a discussion of the lack of provision of infrastructure in India.

21. See Psacharopoulos (1988).

22. See Krueger and Turan (1992) for further discussion.

23. Díaz-Alejandro (1975).

24. See Prebisch (1984) for a retrospective account of the evolution of his views.

25. See Okyar (1965) for a description.

26. See Lewis (1977) for an exposition.

27. There were many countries that perceived themselves as underdeveloped, and later as developing, that had not in fact been colonies. However, there was a widespread view, particu-

larly in Latin America, that the industrialized countries had made the poor nations "economic colonies" even when there were putative national governments. It seems clear that resentment of foreigners and their influence was a major factor in the Chinese revolution, as well as in the politics of Latin America in the postwar period.

28. However, it was implicitly assumed that industrialization was synonymous with economic growth and rising living standards. It was not recognized that there might be a conflict between industrialization—or at least with the means chosen for industrialization—and attaining rapid economic growth. See, for example, the discussion in Bates (1981).

29. Perhaps the most articulate expressions of these views—at least as communicated to those in the industrial countries—originated in India. One of the most moving accounts is that of Nehru (1941).

30. I am indebted to the Institute for Policy Reform for support in the research underlying this section. The material presented here is a condensed version of a longer paper: Anne O. Krueger, "Ideas underlying Development Policy," paper prepared for the Institute for Policy Reform, March 1991.

31. See, for example, World Bank (1986), for an exposition of the role of "taxation of agriculture" in economic development. However, by the 1960s, a number of "dual economy" models and other expositions noted the need for agricultural development as a prerequisite for rapid growth of industry. See also Lewis (1977).

32. An early articulation of the need for industrialization through import substitution may be found in Rosenstern-Rodan (1943).

33. See Baldwin (1969) for an exposition of the argument and a critical analysis of the circumstances under which it might be correct. Even those who are normally closely identified with the neoclassical viewpoint accepted the infant-industry exception as a practical concern in the 1950s. See the quotation from Haberler below.

34. This fall might result from "Learning by Doing" (Arrow 1962), from the training and greater experience of workers, from reaching a sufficient scale of operations, or from other factors. Baldwin's (1969) skeptical analysis of the likelihood that protection

would induce the anticipated response in the face of forms of externalities or market imperfections normally alleged is the classic.

35. Haberler (1988), pp. 50–51. In his introduction to the reprinted Cairo Lectures, Haberler notes that he now believes, in hindsight, that he "went too far . . . in trying to find justification for a certain amount of protectionism in the LDCs." (p. 11)

36. For a review and critical analysis of the "elasticity pessimism" literature, see Radetzki (1990) and the references therein. On "immiserizing growth," see Bhagwati (1987), chs. 3, 4, 5, and 6.

37. For a brief review of this literature, and an examination of the factual basis for it, see Spraos (1980). W. Arthur Lewis (1949, 1969) challenged this proposition, even in the 1950s, and concluded that the terms of trade between primary commodities and manufactures had hardly changed.

38. In addition to the belief that primary commodity prices were inexorably trending downward, the experience of the Great Depression led to the view that they were unstable. That too impelled a desire to move away from "dependence" on primary commodity exports. For a discussion of the impact on policy, see Corbo (1991).

39. See Prebisch (1984), pp. 176ff for a clear retrospective statement of his view.

40. Lewis (1984), p. 127, also noted the possibility of real wage rigidities.

41. See Bhagwati and Srinivasan (1975) for an analysis of how elasticity pessimism affected India and resulted in a self-fulfilling prophesy as the contraction of export supply resulted in a reduced share of world exports for the major primary commodities that India exported.

42. See Lewis (1954) for a fuller exposition of this view.

43. In some countries this issue was avoided by deciding that government-owned enterprises should start production of industrial commodities previously imported. Bureaucrats who are operating parastatal enterprises, however, have the same interests in convincing other officials of their likely future performance as

do private entrepreneurs. Moreover, the high costs of public sector production have been a major source of difficulty for developing countries. In Turkey, public sector enterprises use three to four times as much of both capital *and* labor as private sector enterprises in the same lines of activity. See Krueger and Tuncer (1982).

44. For a statement as to the equivalence of an ideal market outcome and a socialist outcome, see Lippincott (1938). See also Lerner (1944).

45. See Prebisch (1984) for one account.

46. See United Nations (1951) for a representative statement of thought at the time.

47. Government of India, *Second Five Year Plan*, 1956–61. Government of India, New Delhi.

48. It was always recognized that maximizing the growth rate would not be an appropriate objective of economic policy because the implied cost in terms of present consumption would be higher than the social rate of time preference. However, as is discussed later in this chapter, it was felt that private citizens had "too high" a rate of time preference, and that the government, as benevolent guardian, would normally be expected to raise the rate of economic growth above that which would have occurred under laissez-faire by taxing to raise the overall savings rate.

49. These rural credit institutions in fact proved to be uneconomic almost everywhere, and allocated subsidized credits largely to large landowners. See Ruttan (1989) pp. 162–64. It has also been shown that "interconnected" factor markets (for land, rural labor, credit, and agricultural inputs) may be an appropriate mechanism in the presence of informational asymmetries. See, for example, Hoff and Stiglitz (1990) and other articles in the September 1990 *World Bank Economic Review* "Symposium on Imperfect Information and Rural Credit Markets."

50. It was also assumed that government officials would appropriately correct income distribution in line with social preferences and that intervention for that purpose could be accomplished with few deleterious effects on the efficiency of resource allocation. In many countries marginal rates of taxation on incomes subject to

taxes (those of urban wage earners, civil servants, managers of large enterprises) rapidly rose to confiscatory levels and constituted a major factor in the rapid growth of the underground economy. In India the marginal rate of taxation on personal income rose to 95 percent at an income of approximately $3,000 annually.

There was also a line of thought that concluded that there need not be any essential difference between the behavior of privately owned enterprises and public sector enterprises. Thus in some cases it was not even deemed essential that there be "market failure" before public sector enterprises were established. For a statement that the public-private distinction does not matter, see Tinbergen (1984), p. 326: ". . . efficiency considerations need not be a stumbling block if public enterprise is chosen as a means for furthering a country's development. Rather, the nonavailability of sufficiently large private capital is the decisive point."

51. See Becker (1983) for an analysis.

52. Mancur Olson (1965) focussed upon the free-rider problem as one reason why policies inconsistent with Pareto-optimal allocation of resources may occur.

53. It has been argued that if competitive returns accrue to rent seekers, they may be indifferent to the policy's continuation. That assumes costless reallocations, and no uncertainty.

54. It may be inquired as to why, if a leader such as Nehru was genuinely committed to the well-being of the Indian people, he adhered to policies that were manifestly failing in achieving his goals. The answer would appear to lie in two phenomena: First, it took a long period of time before the evidence was clear-cut that the policies were not efficient in achieving their objectives, but also the political-economic interactions described in the next chapter resulted in an evolution of the governmental type and an erosion of Nehru's freedom of maneuver.

55. The quote is from Lal and Myint (1990), p. 465, of their manuscript. They in turn quoted Sabine (1951), p. 721.

56. Findlay (1988), p. 84, has described the outcome of agricultural pricing policies in many countries as follows: "In practice . . . the outcome has been very different. For one thing, the price squeeze [on agriculture] has gone beyond any rational 'optimal

monopsony' level. . . . Thus not only output, but even govern-ment revenue, is probably lower than it would be under a more rational policy. The expenditure, on the other hand, has fre-quently simply gone into the private consumption of the urban beneficiaries or into armaments and other 'public goods' of du-bious social value."

57. Lal and Myint (1990), p. 467.

58. It may be noted that these same governmental forms might also be consistent with the behavior of a benevolent social guard-ian. The distinction lies in the objectives of the dictator, monarch, charismatic leader, or colonial government.

59. See Findlay and Wilson (1987) for a full discussion.

60. Findlay (1988), p. 88.

61. Bates (1983), ch. 3.

62. See Krueger and Turan (1993) for a discussion.

63. Panterritorial pricing of commodities is a widely encountered problem in developing countries. It results in major inefficiencies in the allocation of transport resources, quite aside from other difficulties of a bureaucracy in maintaining a transport system. Incentives are especially low for railroads to schedule pickups and delivery from distant areas, and service can be highly unre-liable. See Jansen (1989) for an account of the difficulties in Zam-bia.

Late delivery of fertilizer is apparently a widespread difficulty of agricultural marketing boards in developing countries. While I was at the World Bank, there were numerous stories of deliveries so far into the planting season that fertilizer could not then be used, and then was greatly reduced in effectiveness because of rain and other damage before the next growing season.

64. Olgun (1991).

65. Olgun (1991) reports that, at one point, Turkish politicians decided that there should be government procurement of pota-toes and onions, and the appropriate government agency was ordered to purchase them. However, the agency had no storage facilities and had to rent warehouses from private parties. There were evidently no mechanisms for marketing the onions and po-tatoes because they eventually rotted in these private ware-houses.

66. See Klitgaard (1990), p. 108, for an account of this problem in equatorial Guinea. A lack of technicians resulted in an inability to repair equipment, and three of the four main generators were not functioning at the time about which Klitgaard reports.

67. This happened because of the need for jobs to extend political patronage, as discussed earlier. But in general bureaucratic managers of more employees are regarded as being "higher up" in the hierarchy than those with fewer employees. In addition it was sometimes a "noneconomic" objective to maintain employment. In Turkey, for example, it was widely believed that all college graduates should locate employment; those who did not find work in the private sector were hired by State Economic Enterprises.

68. See Krueger (1975) for a detailed description of DGTD, the Indian import licensing agency. There officials checked specifications on upwards of 2,000 different items to be imported in connection with construction of factories and importation of equipment for different projects. Delays in issuing import licenses could often exceed two years in order for these inspections to occur.

69. Focus here is on political-economic interactions involving the trade and payments regime. Earlier analysis of their economic effects may be found in Bhagwati (1978), Krueger (1978), and Little, Scitovsky, and Scott (1970).

70. See Nurkse (1953).

71. Brazil also established parastatal enterprises, of which the steel complex is perhaps the best known. However, the fraction of new import-substituting activity in the Brazilian public sector—as in most of Latin America—was probably far smaller than in the countries mentioned above. See Cardoso and Fishlow (1990) for a summary of the Brazilian trade regime.

72. It should also be noted that failing to alter the exchange rate required no action; an exchange rate change entailed a visible public action. In a sense failing to devalue was not a conscious policy decision.

73. When in 1958 there was a devaluation, supported by an IMF program, the official exchange rate was changed from TL2.80 per U.S. dollar to TL9.00 per dollar. See Krueger (1974), p. 34, for more details.

74. Data are from International Monetary Fund, *International Financial Statistics*, p. 249. December 1991.

75. In the economics literature, "foreign exchange shortage" from such regimes was modeled by Chenery and his associates in the famous "two-gap" model of development, in which a constraint upon imports served as a separate bottleneck to growth. See, for example, Chenery and Strout (1966).

76. In some countries exports were diverted from official channels to extralegal ones. Smuggling sometimes became very large, as goods were transported across borders to countries where the real prices were considerably higher.

77. Resistance to devaluation also originated, at least in the 1950s and 1960s, in the ideas of the time. In part this resistance was based on nationalistic considerations in the days in which a stable currency value was regarded as a symptom of nationhood. However, "benevolent social guardian" considerations were also evoked: Based on the then-current thinking about the importance of investment for development, it was everywhere noted that devaluation would make imported capital goods more expensive and thus "discourage" investment. That the importation of capital goods would in any event be limited by the available foreign exchange was little noticed.

78. These same mechanisms also provided incentives for use of capital-using technology, as the overvalued exchange rate made imports of machinery and equipment relatively inexpensive for those who could obtain it. The fact that much of the "formal sector" industry was relatively capital intensive reinforced the power of labor unions to extract relatively large wage increases.

79. See Krueger (1975) for particulars.

80. Indirect policy instruments are defined as those that are not directly aimed at prices of agricultural inputs and outputs or at farmers' incomes but that nonetheless have a significant impact on the returns to agriculture. The two major indirect policies are maintenance of a nominal exchange rate despite rapid domestic inflation and protection of import-competing industries producing agricultural inputs or items farmers consume. See Schiff and Valdés (1992) for a discussion.

81. See World Bank (1986) for an analysis of implicit and explicit taxation of agriculture and its effects.

82. It was not until T. W. Schultz's (1964) pioneering work that this notion was challenged. Even then, attacks against the notion of a creative industrious peasant, responsive to incentives, were widespread. See the discussion in Krueger, Ruttan, and Michalopoulos (1989), pp. 18ff.

83. In the industrial countries it is widely believed that a major motive for the developing countries' agricultural pricing policies has been to "improve the income distribution." In practice there has been very little redistribution relative to the deadweight costs. Such redistribution as there has been has typically been away from the rural poor and toward the urban middle and upper income groups. In none of the countries other than Egypt covered by the Agricultural Pricing Project was the income distribution consequence of agricultural pricing policies in the presumed direction.

84. Urban wage earners included civil servants and employees of parastatal enterprises.

85. In some countries such as Thailand the export crops were also the major food crops. In other countries the food crops were import substituting, while export crops were not significant food items. In the latter case the attempt to provide cheap urban food either constituted a drain upon foreign exchange earnings (as in Egypt where wheat was imported and consumption heavily subsidized) or food crops were accorded high levels of domestic protection, with a consequent pull of resources away from export crops. Either way, the inconsistencies were still a major source of tension, as described below.

86. See Bates (1989).

87. See Stryker (1990) and Bates (1983) for an account of the transformation of the Cocoa Marketing Board in Ghana.

88. See Stryker (1990).

89. See Jansen (1988).

90. See Fernando (1987) for an excellent description of the changes in laws and administrative arrangements that accompanied the

efforts of the Sri Lankan government to distribute agricultural inputs and outputs.

91. See note 2 for the definition of "direct" and "indirect" policies.

92. It is interesting that despite this "power" Garcia concluded that there had been direct, as well as indirect, discrimination against coffee. Garcia (1991), p. 153.

93. See Krueger (1992), ch. 6.

94. Korea was an exception after the early 1970s. Prior to that date Korean economic policies were similar to those described here.

95. In addition in both Sri Lanka and Malaysia rice was grown by those associated with the political party in power. See the subsequent discussion.

96. An interesting partial exception appears to have been Egypt in the latter half of the 1980s. See the fascinating analysis in Holt and Roe (1993).

97. See Bhagwati and Srinivasan (1975), pp. 126ff.

98. See, for example, Santhanam Committee (1964).

99. *Economist*, December 7, 1991, Brazil Survey, p. 7.

100. See Lal and Maxfield (1993) and Cardoso (1991) for accounts.

101. Data are based on the consumer price index as reported in the International Monetary Fund, *International Monetary Fund*, December 1991, p. 71.

102. This need not inexorably continue. There are several possible alternatives: A democratically elected charismatic leader could assume office and undertake a successful and meaningful reform program; there could be a change in form of government; even a new finance minister, such as happened in Argentina, could begin to reverse the process. The Argentine experience would suggest that once inflation has reached the Brazilian-Argentina heights, there is a strong political reward (i.e., popular support) for those who can sharply reduce it.

103. See Krueger and Turan (1993) for an analysis of the three episodes, and the similarity in their origins. The political-eco-

nomic structure and interaction were much the same in the earlier periods. After 1980, however, the change in economic policies led to a very different economic-political evolution than had the earlier programs. The following discussion is based upon the analysis in Krueger and Turan (1993).

104. Although the rate of inflation fell from over 100 percent at its peak to 35 percent in 1982, the Turkish economy remained inflation prone throughout the 1980s. Analysis of the political-economic reasons for the persistence of inflationary difficulties is not germane to the discussion here. It should be noted, however, that by the end of the decade, the sources of support that the government received because of the success of its earlier economic policies eroded as inflation persisted.

105. Autonomy was not complete, for governmental spending rose sharply before each election with inflationary consequences afterward. But spending and consequent fiscal deficits resulted in a resumption of accelerating inflation, and with the inflation, an erosion of the political base of the regime. See Krueger and Turan (1992) for an analysis.

106. See Cole and Lyman (1971) for particulars.

107. When terms of trade improved for individual developing countries, there immediately followed the inevitable political pressures to increase government expenditures. When commodity prices predictably fell thereafter, it normally proved politically infeasible to reduce governmental expenditures in anything like the same proportion.

108. An important question is why inflation is politically acceptable in differing degrees in different countries. While there are some obvious parts to the answer—the degree of indexation of the economy, the degree to which influential groups are directly harmed or benefited by inflation, and past historical experience—there does not as yet appear to be a fully satisfactory explanation of why the Asian subcontinent was so much more concerned about inflation than was most of Latin America.

109. In a strict scientific sense it is impossible to generalize about "crises." A major problem is that there is no empirically observable widely accepted definition of what is, and what is not, a crisis. What would be a crisis rate of inflation in Turkey, for ex-

ample, would not be so regarded in Brazil. Conversely, the Turkish political process has typically responded to balance-of-payments difficulties in circumstances in which the government of India has simply tightened foreign exchange controls and accepted the higher economic costs of that alternative. The situation gets confounded further when it is recognized that stagnant living standards can be seen as an imperative for action in some countries (e.g., Turkey) and not in others (e.g., Myanmar).

110. See Kraft (1984) for an account.

111. The term is due to Deepak Lal.

112. It is at least conceivable that there was a "window of opportunity" for a far-reaching set of policy changes at the time the first Cruzado Plan was announced. As shown by Cardoso (1991), that plan as implemented had no chance of success because underlying fiscal imbalances were not addressed.

113. However, the new government simultaneously embarked upon a very expansionist macroeconomic program.

114. See Hamid, Nabi, and Nasim (1991) for an account.

115. See Corbo and de Melo (1987) for an analysis of the Chilean case, and Edwards (1989), pp. 57ff, for an analysis of the Argentine case.

116. See Krueger and Turan (1992) for a detailed account.

117. See, for example, the data in Krueger (1978) and Edwards (1989).

118. For analyses of the determinants, see Krueger (1992), Michaely, Papageorgiou, and Choksi (1991), and McKinnon (1992).

119. This is not to argue that the multilateral lending institutions do not have an important role to play in support of policy reform: they do. But that role is to provide technical support and advice to avoid the sorts of technical mistakes discussed above that can result in failure. An honest evaluation of the adequacy of proposed deficit reductions, of the magnitude of the proposed nominal devaluation, and other key variables, and insistence upon policy changes that are crucial and would otherwise be overlooked, is invaluable in ensuring that "windows of opportunity" are not wasted.

120. Bhagwati (1978) and Krueger (1978).

121. See Schiff and Valdes (1992) and Krueger (1992).

122. See, for example, the collection of essays in Kahler (1986). See also the provocative essay by Grindle (1991).

123. It is often forgotten that the Korean government was elected through an open democratic process in the 1960s: Electoral irregularities did not start until 1972. See Mason et al. (1980), pp. 45ff, for an account.

References

Arrow, Kenneth. 1962. The economic implications of learning by doing. *Review of Economic Studies* 29:155–73.

Baldwin, Robert E. 1969. The case against infant industry protection. *Journal of Political Economy* 77(3):295–305.

Bardhan, Pranab. 1984. *The Political Economy of Development in India.* Oxford: Basil Blackwell.

Bates, Robert H. 1981. *Markets and States in Tropical Africa: The Political Basis of Agricultural Policies.* Berkeley: University of California Press.

Bates, Robert H. 1983. *Essays on the Political Economy of Rural Africa.* Berkeley: University of California Press.

Bates, Robert H. 1989. *Beyond the Miracle of the Market.* Cambridge: Cambridge University Press.

Bates, Robert H., and Paul Collier. 1993. The politics and economics of policy reform in Zambia. In Robert H. Bates and Anne O. Krueger, eds., *Political and Economic Interactions in Economic Policy Reform: Evidence from Eight Countries.* Oxford: Basil Blackwell.

Becker, Gary S. 1983. A theory of competition among pressure groups for political influence. *Quarterly Journal of Economics* 98(3):371–400.

Behrman, Jere R. 1975. *Foreign Trade Regimes and Economic Development. Chile.* New York: Columbia University Press.

Bhagwati, Jagdish N. 1978. *Foreign Trade Regimes and Economic Development: Anatomy and Consequences of Exchange Control Regimes.* Cambridge, MA: Ballinger.

Bhagwati, Jagdish N. 1987. *The Theory of Commercial Policy.* Cambridge, MA: MIT Press.

Bhagwati, Jagdish N., and T. N. Srinivasan. 1975. *Foreign Trade Regimes and Economic Development. India.* New York: Columbia University Press.

Cardenas, Enrique. 1990. Contemporary economic problems in historical perspective. In Dwight S. Brothers and Adele E. Wick, eds., *Mexico's Search for a New Development Strategy.* Boulder: Westview, pp. 1–25.

Cardoso, Eliana. 1991. From inertia to megainflation: Brazil in the 1980s. In Michael Bruno, Stanley Fischer, Elhanan Helpman, and Nissan Liviatan, eds., *Lessons of Economic Stabilization and Its Aftermath.* Cambridge: MIT Press, pp. 1433–77.

Cardoso, Eliana, and Albert Fishlow. 1990. The macroeconomics of the Brazilian external debt. In Jeffrey D. Sachs, ed., *Developing Country Debt and Economic Performance.* Chicago: University of Chicago Press, pp. 269–391.

Carvalho, José L., and Claudio L. S. Haddad. 1981. Foreign trade strategies and employment in Brazil. In Anne O. Krueger, Hal B. Lary, and Narongchai Akrasanee, eds., *Trade and Employment in Developing Countries. 1. Individual Studies.* Chicago: University of Chicago Press, pp. 29–82.

Chenery, Hollis B., and Alan Strout. 1966. Foreign assistance and economic development. *American Economic Review* 56(4):679–733.

Cole, David, and Princeton Lyman. 1971. *Korean Development, The Interplay of Politics and Economics,* Cambridge, MA: Harvard University Press.

Corbo, Vittorio. 1991. Development strategies and policies in Latin America: A historical perspective. World Bank, February, pp. 4–5.

Corbo, Vittorio, and Jaime de Melo. 1987. Lessons from the southern cone policy reforms. *World Bank Research Observer* 2(2):111–42.

Díaz-Alejandro, Carlos. 1975. *Foreign Trade Regimes and Economic Development. Colombia.* New York: Columbia University Press.

De Soto, Hernando. 1989. *The Other Path.* New York: Harper and Row.

Edwards, Sebastian. 1989. *Real Exchange Rates, Devaluation, and Adjustment.* Cambridge, MA: MIT Press.

Fernando, Nimal. 1987. Agricultural pricing policy in Sri Lanka. Mimeo. World Bank.

Fernando, Nimal. 1988. The political economy of Mahaweli. Mimeo. World Bank.

Findlay, Ronald. 1988. Trade, development, and the state. In Gustav Ranis and T. Paul Schultz, eds., *The State of Development Economics. Progress and Perspectives.* Oxford: Basil Blackwell, pp. 78–95.

Findlay, Ronald, and John D. Wilson. 1987. The political economy of Leviathan. In Assaf Razin and Efraim Sadka, eds., *Economic Policy in Theory and Practice.* London: Macmillan.

Garcia, Jorge Garcia, 1991. The political economy of agricultural pricing in Colombia. In Anne O. Krueger, Maurice Schiff, and Alberto Valdés, eds., *The Political Economy of Agricultural Pricing Policies.* Vol. 1: *Latin America.* Baltimore: Johns Hopkins University Press.

Grindle, Merilee S. 1991. The new political economy: Positive economics and negative politics. In Gerald M. Meier, ed., *Politics and Policy Making in Developing Countries.* San Francisco: Institute for Contemporary Studies, pp. 41–68.

Haberler, Gottfried. 1959. *The Cairo Lectures: International Trade and Economic Development.* Reprinted in his *International Trade and Economic Development,* 1988. San Francisco: Center for International Economic Growth.

Hamid, Naved, Ijaz Nabi, and Anjum Nasim. 1991. Pakistan. In Anne O. Krueger, Maurice Schiff, and Alberto Valdés, eds., *The Political Economy of Agricultural Pricing Policy.* Vol. 2: *Asia.* Baltimore: Johns Hopkins University Press, pp. 107–48.

Hansen, Bent. 1975. *Foreign Trade Regimes and Economic Development: Egypt.* New York: Columbia University Press.

Hansen, Bent. 1992. *The Political Economy of Poverty, Equity, and Growth: Egypt and Turkey*. Oxford: Oxford University Press.

Hoff, Karla, and Joseph E. Stiglitz. 1990. Introduction: Imperfect information and rural credit markets—Puzzles and policy perspectives. *World Bank Economic Review* 4(3):235–50.

Holt, Robert E., and Terry Roe. 1993. The Political Economy of Policy Reform in Egypt. In Robert H. Bates and Anne O. Krueger, eds., *Political and Economic Interactions in Economic Policy Reform: Evidence from Eight Countries*. Oxford: Basil Blackwell.

Jansen, Doris. 1988. *Trade, Exchange Rates, and Agricultural Pricing Policies in Zambia*. Washington, DC: World Bank.

Kahler, Miles. ed. 1986. *The Politics of International Debt*. Ithaca: Cornell University Press.

Kaufman, Robert R. 1988. *The Politics of Debt in Argentina, Brazil and Mexico*. Berkeley: University of California Press.

Klitgaard, Robert. 1990. *Tropical Gangsters*. New York: Basic Books.

Kraft, Joseph. 1984. *The Mexican Rescue*. New York: Group of Thirty.

Krueger, Anne O. 1974. *Foreign Trade Regimes and Economic Development: Turkey*. New York: Columbia University Press.

Krueger, Anne O. 1975. *The Benefits and Costs of Import Substitution in India: A Microeconomic Study*. Minneapolis: University of Minnesota Press.

Krueger, Anne O. 1978. *Foreign Trade Regimes and Economic Development: Liberalization Attempts and Consequences*. Cambridge, MA: Ballinger.

Krueger, Anne O. 1983. *Alternative Trade Strategies and Employment*. Vol. 3: *Synthesis*. Chicago: University of Chicago Press.

Krueger, Anne O. 1988. The Relationship between Trade, Employment and Development. In Gustav Ranis and T. Paul Schultz, eds., *The State of Development Economics*. Oxford: Basil Blackwell, pp. 357–84.

Krueger, Anne O. 1992. *The Political Economy of Agricultural Pricing Policies*. Vol. 5: *Synthesis*. Baltimore: Johns Hopkins University Press.

Krueger, Anne O., and Okan Aktan. 1992. *Swimming against the Tide: Turkish Trade Reform in the 1980s*. San Francisco: Institute for Contemporary Studies.

Krueger, Anne O., Vernon Ruttan, and Constantine Michalopoulos. 1989. *Aid and Development*. Baltimore: Johns Hopkins University Press.

Krueger, Anne O., Maurice Schiff, and Alberto Valdés. 1988. Agricultural incentives in developing countries: Measuring the effect of sectoral and economywide policies. *World Bank Economic Review* 2(3):255–71.

Krueger, Anne O., and Baran Tuncer. 1982. An empirical test of the infant industry argument. *American Economic Review* 72:1142–52.

Krueger, Anne O., and Ilter Turan. 1993. "The political economy of economic policy reform in Turkey. In Robert E. Bates and Anne O. Krueger, eds., *Political and Economic Interactions in Economic Policy Reform: Evidence from Eight Countries*. Oxford: Basil Blackwell.

Lal, Deepak, and Sylvia Maxfield. 1993. The political economy of policy reform in Brazil. In Robert Bates and Anne O. Krueger, eds., *Political and Economic Interactions in Economic Policy Reform: Evidence from Eight Countries*. Oxford: Basil Blackwell.

Lal, Deepak, and Hla Myint. 1990. *Poverty, Equity and Economic Growth*. Mimeo. World Bank Comparative Study. Washington, DC.

Lerner, Abba P. 1944. *The Economics of Control*. New York: Macmillan.

Lewis, W. Arthur. 1949. *Economic Survey*. London: Allen and Unwin.

Lewis, W. Arthur. 1954. Economic development with unlimited supplies of labour. Reprinted in A. N. Agarwala and S. P. Singh, eds., *The Economics of under Development*. Oxford: Oxford University Press, 1963, pp. 400–49.

Lewis, W. Arthur. 1969. *Aspects of Tropical Trade, 1883–1965*. Stockholm: Almqvist and Wiksell.

Lewis, W. Arthur. 1977. *The Evolution of the International Economic Order*. Princeton: Princeton University Press.

Lewis, W. Arthur. 1984. Development economics in the 1950s. In Gerald M. Meier and Dudley Seers, eds., *Pioneers in Development*. Oxford: Oxford University Press, p. 127.

Lippincott, B. 1938. *On the Economic Theory of Socialism*. Minneapolis: University of Minnesota Press.

Little, I. M. D., Tibor Scitovsky, and Maurice Scott. 1970. *Industry and Trade in Some Developing Countries*. Oxford: Oxford University Press.

MacKenzie, G. A. 1989. Are all summary indicators of the stance of fiscal policy misleading? *International Monetary Fund Staff Papers* 36(4):743–70.

Mason, Edward S., Dwight H. Perkins, Kwang Suk Kim, and David C. Cole. 1980. *The Economic and Social Modernization of the Republic of Korea*. Cambridge: Harvard University Press.

McKinnon, Ronald I. 1991. *The Order of Economic Liberalization: Financial Control in the Transition to a Market Economy*. Baltimore: Johns Hopkins University Press.

Michaely, Michael, Demetris Papageorgiou, and Armeane M. Choksi. 1991. *Liberalizing Foreign Trade*, vol. 7. Oxford: Basil Blackwell.

Myrdal, Gunnar. 1968. *Asian Drama: An Inquiry into the Poverty of Nations*. London: Allen Lane.

Nehru, Jawaharlal. 1941. *Toward Freedom*. Boston: Beacon Press.

Nurkse, Ragnar. 1953. *Problems of Capital Formation in Developing Countries*. Oxford: Basil Blackwell.

Okyar, Osman. 1965. The concept of etatism. *Economic Journal* 75(297):98–111.

Olgun, Hasan. 1991. Turkey. In Anne O. Krueger, Maurice Schiff, and Alberto Valdés, eds., *The Political Economy of Agricultural Pricing Policy*. Vol. 3: *Africa and the Mediterranean*. Baltimore: Johns Hopkins University Press, pp. 230–67.

Olson, Mancur. 1965. *The Logic of Collective Action*. Cambridge: Harvard University Press.

Prebisch, Raul. 1984. Five stages in my thinking on development.

In Gerald M. Meier and Dudley Seers, eds., *Pioneers in Development*. Washington, DC: World Bank, 1984, pp. 175–91.

Psacharaopoulos, George. 1988. Education and development: A review. *World Bank Research Observer* 3(1):99–115.

Radetzki, Marian. 1990. *A Guide to Primary Commodities in the World Economy*. Oxford: Basil Blackwell.

Rosenstern-Rodan, P. N. 1943. Problems of industrialization in eastern and southeastern Europe. *Economic Journal* 53:202–11.

Ruttan, Vernon. 1989. Assistance to expand agricultural production. In Anne O. Krueger, Vernon W. Ruttan, and Constantine Michalopoulos, eds., *Aid and Development*. Baltimore: Johns Hopkins University Press, ch. 9.

Sabine, G. H. 1951. *A History of Political Theory*. London: Harrap.

Santhanam Committee. 1964. *Report of the Committee on Prevention of Corruption*. New Delhi: Government of India, Ministry of Home Affairs.

Schiff, Maurice, and Alberto Valdés. 1993. *The Political Economy of Agricultural Pricing Policies in Developing Countries*. Vol. 4: *A Synthesis of the Economics in Developing Countries*. Baltimore: Johns Hopkins University Press.

Schultz, Theodore W. 1964. *Transforming Traditional Agriculture*. New Haven: Yale University Press.

Spraos, John. 1980. The statistical debate on the net barter terms of trade between primary commodities and manufactures. *Economic Journal* 90:97–128.

Stryker, J. Dirck. 1990. *Trade, Exchange Rate, and Agricultural Pricing Policies in Ghana*. World Bank Comparative Studies. Washington, DC: World Bank.

Tinbergen, Jan. 1984. Development Cooperation as a Learning Process. In Gerald M. Meier and Dudley Seers, eds., *Pioneers in Development*. Oxford: Oxford University Press, pp. 315–31.

United Nations Department of Economic Affairs. 1951. *Measures for the Economic Development of Underdeveloped Countries*. New York.

World Bank. 1986. *World Development Report*. Oxford: Oxford University Press.

Index

Absolutist, 61
Administrative capacity, 66–73
Africa, 2, 39–40, 76, 123, 128. *See
also specific African countries*
Agricultural Marketing Boards
(AMBs), 92–98, 97–98, 100, 108
Agricultural pricing policies, 91–92
   direct vs. indirect, 101–102
   impact of, 22–24
   market response to, 96–98
   origins of, 92–95
   political reactions and, 98–101
   questions for political economy
   and, 101–106
Agricultural producers' associations, 102
Agriculture
   controls, market controls and,
   106
   distribution systems, 96–97
   exports, 103–104
   import-competing, 103–104
   industrialization and, 93
   political objectives and, 94
   quality grading of commodities,
   26
   taxation of, 93, 103–105
Anticolonialism, 39
Anti-inflation programs, 32–33
Argentina
   agricultural import/export mix,
   105
   as bureaucratic-authoritarian factional state, 63
   economic difficulties in 1908, 12
   food imports, 98
   inflation, 123
   reforms, 124–125, 129–132
   stop-go cycle and, 35
Argentina Central Bank, 27
Asia, 1–2, 39–40, 51
Atatürk, Kemal, 61
Austerity, 32–33
Authoritarian states, 89
Autonomous states, 59, 61, 64, 113

Benevolent social guardians
   administrative capacity and, 66–
   67
   government as, 54–59
   influence on economic policies,
   38
   labor market regulations, 107
   reforms, 118
   transition to bureaucratic-authoritarian state, 139–140
   transition to bureaucratic-autonomous state, 86, 88
Bhutto, Ali, 129
Black markets, 12, 20, 33, 78, 81,
   83, 99, 110
Bolivia, 13
Brazil
   agricultural import/export mix,
   105
   anti-inflation plans, 33
   constraints, political structure
   and, 60

Brazil (continued)
  credit subsidies to farmers, 27
  economic deterioration, 13
  import substitution and, 76
  inflation, 123
  political-economic interactions,
    sequence of, 114–116
  real exchange rates, 20
  reforms, 124–125, 128, 131, 137
  stop-go cycle and, 35
Bribery, 82–83, 97, 113
Bureaucracy, 87–88, 113
Bureaucratic-authoritarian states,
  61, 63, 126, 140
Bureaucratic-autonomous states,
  86
Bureaucratic predatory states, 89
Bureaucratic states, 113

Capital-intensive techniques, 22,
  27
Capital–labor ratios, 27–28
Chile, 20, 30, 33, 127, 130–131,
  139–140
Civil servants, 57
Coalitions, 65, 87, 139–140
Coffee Growers' Association, 102
Colombia, 34–35, 40, 89, 102, 104
Corruption, of government offi-
  cials, 113
Credit rationing, 107
Creditworthiness, 122
Crisis, determination of, 124–125
Cruzado Plan, 33, 130–131

Debt, of developing countries in
  1980s, 1–3
Debt crisis, 1
Debt–service ratios, 2–3
Debt servicing, 18
Demirel, Prime Minister S., 12, 117
Developing countries. See also
  specific countries
  agricultural discrimination, 92
  changes in government, policy
    change and, 128–129
  debt in 1980s, 1–3
  development, achievement of
    equality and, 41
  distribution systems, 68–71

economic policies in, 11–35
economic structures of, 40–41
evolution of policy, 37
ex-colonial legacy, 39–40
exploitation of, 42
fertilizer marketing, 68–70
government expenditures, 18
government intervention in, 55
growth in 1980s, 1–2
high flyers, economic policies of,
  29–35
high-inflation experiences in,
  15–17
ideas underlying industrialization in, 43–48
inports and, 75
import substitution, encouragement of, 76–77
initial conditions for policy formulation, 39–42
labor supply in, 47
macroeconomic instability, 15–19
mining in, 24–25
origins of policy, 38–39
political economy of policy determination, 9
reform in, 136
role of government in economy,
  48–51
"self-view" of citizens, 40–41
trade and exchange rate policies,
  19–28
Dictatorships, 60
Discrimination, agricultural, 103–
  105, 129
Distribution systems, 68–71, 96–97
Domestic policies, 19

East Asian countries, growth in
  1980s, 1–2
Eastern Europe, 119
Economic policy. See Policy
Economic-political interaction, 139
Education expenditures, 28
Egypt, 23, 98, 100, 104–106, 124,
  133
European Common Agricultural
  Policy, 14
Exchange rates
  black market, 12, 20

exchange controls and, 20
nominal, 19, 77, 97
overvaluation, 20–22
real, 20, 77–78, 82–83, 108
Expenditures, imbalance with revenues, 121–122
Exports
agricultural, 103–104
incentives, 19
of primary commodities, pessimism of, 43, 46–47
subsidies, 21
External shocks, 137

Factional states, 59, 65–66, 87, 105, 133
Factor market policies, 26–27
Fertilizer marketing, in developing countries, 68–70
Food crops, low consumer prices for, 23
Food price subsidies, 93–94, 100–101
Foreign assistance, 120
Foreign borrowing, from private sources, 122
Foreign exchange
costs, 98
receipts, 20
reserves, 78–79, 84–85
shortages, 32–35, 108
Foreign resources, 122
Foreign trade regimes, evolution of, 136–137
Free-rider problems, 57–59

Gabon, 18
Gandhi, Prime Minister Rajiv, 113–114
Garcia, Alain, 132
Ghana, 12, 40, 65, 78, 91, 98, 104–105, 124, 131
Government
alternative models, 59–66
as benevolent social guardian
(see Benevolent social guardians) economic policies and, 139
efficiency, policy and, 53–54
expenditures in developing countries, 18

industry and, 23
organizations, 25
perceptions of, reform success and, 134
policies, farmers and, 23–24
policy cycles and, 9–11
role in economy of developing countries, 48–51
type, reforms and, 126
Government officials
connections with, 82
corruption of, 113
incentives for, 71
Gray markets, 107–108
Great Depression, 39, 41–43
Growth
as conscious policy objective, 40
deceleration, 119–121
of developing countries in 1980s, 1–2
immiserizing, 47
Guardian states, 61–62

"Hard" states, 139
Hee, Park Chung, 118
Hong Kong, 30
Hwan, Chun Doo, 118

Import-competing agriculture, 103–104
Import licensing, 78–86, 89
Import restrictions, 19
Import substitution, 87, 107
encouragement of, 76–77
industrialization and, 43, 45–47
Incentives
for capital-intensive techniques, 22
for civil servants, 71–72
for government officials, 71
for labor-saving techniques, 22
India
as benevolent social guardian, 61
devaluation, 21
import licenses, 76–77
import-substitution policies, 87
living standards, 40
parastatals, 24–25
private sector controls, 28
reforms, 124, 131, 133

India (continued)
  sequences of political-economic
    interaction, 109–114
  transition to bureaucratic-auton-
    omous state, 86
Indian Five-Year Plans, 50–51, 55,
  110
Indonesia, 27, 61, 131
Industrialization
  agriculture and, 93
  drive for, in developing coun-
    tries, 75, 93
  import substitution and, 43, 45–
    47
  of Soviet Union, 39, 42
  underlying ideas, in developing
    countries, 43–48
Infant-industry protection, 43–49,
  75, 89
Inflation
  high, in developing countries,
    15–17
  in policy cycle, 32–33
Informal sector, 82
Information asymmetry, 71–72
Interest groups, 57, 65, 88, 102,
  120
International Monetary Fund
  (IMF), 33–34, 89
  Articles of Agreement, 77
  high-inflation countries, 15–17
  policy reform programs, 4–8
  stabilization program, 124
International trade theory, 45–47
Investment licensing mechanisms,
  110
Ivory Coast, 104–105

Jamaica, 13, 18
Japan, 40, 93

Kenya, 18, 65, 104
Korea
  agricultural import/export mix,
    104
  as benevolent social guardian, 61
  constraints, political structure
    and, 60
  economic policy of, 29–30
  foreign assistance, 120

  foreign resources and, 122
  governmental change, policy
    change and, 118–119
  reforms, 125, 127, 131, 137, 139–
    140

Labor market regulations, 27,
  107
Labor-saving techniques, incen-
  tives, 22
Labor supply, in developing
  countries, 47
Labor union leaders, trade and
  payments regime and, 86
Labor unions, 114–115
Latin America, 64, 119
  growth in 1980s, 2
  policy-making cycles, 135–136
  public sector deficit, 18
Law of Similars, 76
Leviathan state, 63–64
Liberia, 18
Lobbies, 57

Macroeconomic policy, instability,
  in developing countries, 15–19
Malaysia, 65, 105
Malthusian doctrine, 46
Market controls, agriculture controls and, 106
Market failures, 49, 53, 56
Marketing, in developing countries, 68–70
Marketing Boards. See Agricultural Marketing Boards
Market response, to government
  agricultural pricing policies, 96–
  98
Mexico
  balance-of-payments crisis in
    1982, 11
  borrowing from private sources,
    122
  fiscal deficit, 18
  government expenditures, 18
  reforms, 123, 131, 140
Mining, in developing countries,
  24–25
Monopolies and Restrictive Practices Commission, 111

Morocco, 18, 98

Nationalism, 39, 41, 76
Negative exports, 21
Nehru, Jawaharlal, 61
New Guinea, 27
Niger, 13
Nigeria, 21

Oil prices, 1979 increases, 1
Özal, Turgut, 117, 131

Pakistan, 129
Parastatals, 22
  in Africa, 76
  controls on, 28
  economic behavior of, 14
  government planning and, 50
  ill-equipped, 25–26
  macroeconomic problems and,
    26
  mining, 24–25
  problems with, 70–71
  in Turkey, 26, 30–31
Pareto optimum, 56, 66
Peru, 12, 21, 129, 132
Philippines, 13, 27
Policy
  across-the-board difficulties, 13–
    28
  agricultural pricing (see Agricul-
    tural pricing policies)
  categorization of, 14
  choice, 4
  in developing countries, 11–35
  development process, 2, 4
  domestic, 19
  economic efficiency and, 53–54
  evolution, 37
  factor market, 26–27
  governmental change and, 128–
    129
  growth, as conscious objective,
    40
  of high flyers, 29–35
  implementation, 68
  inappropriate, in 1980s, 2
  influence of ideas on, 38
  initial conditions for formulation,
    39–42

objectives, 56
origins, 38
political economy in developing
  countries, 13
reform process, 4
trade and exchange rate, 19–28
type of government and, 139
types, economic activity and,
  13–14
Policy cycle, "stop-go" cycle, 89,
  123–124, 127, 135, 140
Policy-making cycles, 135–138
  foreign exchange-induced, 32–35
  government and, 9–11
  inflation-induced, 32–34
  types of, 31–35
Political-economic interaction,
  107–109
  buildup to economic crisis, 119–
    124
  evolution of, 138–141
  macroeconomic, sequences of,
    109–119
  nature of reforms, 129–132
  reform decisions, 124–129
  success of reforms and, 132–134
  ultimate, 109
Political institutions, democratization of, 140–141
Politically determined policies,
  economic consequences of,
  9
Political reactions, to agricultural
  pricing policies, 98–101
Portugal, 104
Predatory states, 61–64, 87
Price ceilings, 28
Primary commodities prices, pessimism of, 43, 46–47
Private sector
  controls, 28
  industry, in trade and payments
    regimes, 86–87
  self-interest assumption and, 56–
    57
Protectionism, 21–23
Public savings, increasing, 93
Public sector
  deficit, 18
  enterprises, 19

Public sector (continued)
  investment and maintenance
    programs, 28
  resources, squeeze on, 121
  self-interest assumption and, 57

Rationing, 98
Real exchange rates, 108
  appreciation, 77–78, 82–83
  coefficient of variation, 20
Reform, 35
  governmental types and, 126
  honeymoon period, 127–128
  in Korea, 29–30
  nature of programs, 129–132
  palliative programs, 140
  political economy of policy de-
    termination, 8
  programs, 4–8, 123
  success of programs, 132–134
  windows of opportunity, 131–
    132
Rent seeking, 58, 113
Revenues, imbalance with expenditures, 121–122
Rhee, President Sygman, 122
Rulers. *See also specific rulers*
  constrained power, 64–65
  party, 63
  single, 62–63

Singapore, 20, 30
Smuggling, 20, 22, 81, 83, 85, 99,
  110
Social insurance, 27
"Soft" states, 139
South and Southeastern Asia, 39–
  40, 51. *See also specific Asian
  countries*
South Korea, 12, 37
Soviet Union, industrialization of,
  39–40, 42
Sri Lanka, 18, 20, 99, 105, 128–
  129, 140
Stabilization program, 89, 124
Stop-go cycle, 89, 123–124, 127,
  135, 140
SubSaharan African countries, 2,
  39–40
Sudan, 13, 91, 124

Taiwan, 12, 30, 119, 131, 139–140
Tanzania, 18
Tariff structure, 77
Taxation, of agriculture, 93, 103–
  105
Tax collection systems, 19
Tax structures, 19
Technocrats, 126, 130–131, 138
Thailand, 105
Trade and exchange rate policies,
  in developing countries, 19–
  28
Trade and payments regimes
  evolution of, 85–86, 90, 137
  groups benefiting from, 87–88
  import licensing and, 73–86, 89
  import substitution and, 76–77
  infant-industry argument and,
    75–76
  labor union leaders and, 86
  private sector industry, 86–87
  real exchange rate overvaluation,
    77–78
  rejection of devaluation and, 88
Turkey
  agricultural discrimination, 104–
    106
  as benevolent social guardian
    state, 61
  economic policy in, 12
  exchange rate appreciation, 78–
    80
  as factional state, 66
  foreign exchange, 122–123
  growth as policy objective, 40
  import licensing, 20–21, 76–77
  parastatals, 26, 30–31
  political-economic interactions,
    sequence of, 116–118
  reforms, 124–125, 127–128, 131,
    140
  stabilization program, 34
  tobacco procurement, 70
  transition to bureaucratic-auton-
    omous state, 86

Uganda, 13
Underground economies, 107–108
Uruguay, 98
U.S. fiscal deficits, 14

World Bank, policy reform pro-
    grams, 4–8
World Bank project, 101–102, 104,
    106
World Bank Structural Adjust-
    ment Loan, 99

Zambia, 13, 18, 99–100, 104, 128
Zia ul-Haq, General Mohammed,
    129

DATE DUE

GAYLORD			PRINTED IN U.S.A.